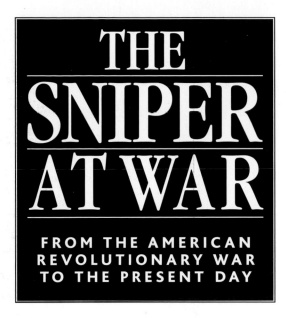

THE SNIPER AT WAR

FROM THE AMERICAN REVOLUTIONARY WAR TO THE PRESENT DAY

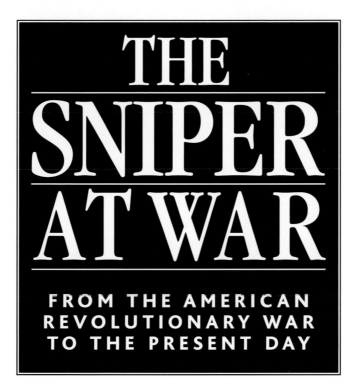

THE SNIPER AT WAR

FROM THE AMERICAN REVOLUTIONARY WAR TO THE PRESENT DAY

MICHAEL E. HASKEW

THOMAS DUNNE BOOKS
ST. MARTIN'S PRESS ❧ NEW YORK

THOMAS DUNNE BOOKS
An imprint of St. Martin's Press

ISBN: 0-312-33651-9

EAN: 978-0312-33651-6

First U.S. Edition 2005

Editorial and design by
Amber Books Ltd
Bradley's Close
74–77 White Lion Street
London N1 9PF
United Kingdom
www.amberbooks.co.uk

Project Editor: Michael Spilling
Copy Editor: Stephen Chumbley
Design: Jerry Williams
Picture Research: Natasha Jones

Printed in Italy

10 9 8 7 6 5 4 3 2 1

CONTENTS

American General Daniel Morgan raised one of the most famous regiments of the Revolutionary War – Morgan's Riflemen – and commanded the Colonists during a brilliant victory at Cowpens on 17 January 1781. Morgan's Riflemen – a contingent of 500 – proved invaluable during the Saratoga campaign.

CHAPTER ONE

THE WARS OF EMPIRE

The keen eye and steady nerve of the accomplished marksman came to the fore during the latter half of the eighteenth century. The genesis of the modern sniper began in earnest during wars waged to gain empire and to achieve independence.

Perhaps the most significant rifle shot in military history is one which was never taken. On 7 September 1777, Major Patrick Ferguson of the King's 70th Foot took aim at an American officer of obviously high rank, who was wearing a large cocked hat and sitting astride a bay horse. As the officer rode along the banks of Brandywine Creek in Pennsylvania, Ferguson contemplated pulling the trigger. He later wrote, '… but it was not pleasant to shoot at the back of an unoffending individual, who was acquitting himself very coolly of his duty; so I let him alone'.

Ferguson was well known in the British Army as a crack shot. He was also keenly aware of the potential value of soldiers who were skilled marksmen. The inventor of a breech-loading rifle which was far more accurate and even lighter in weight than the standard issue Brown Bess musket, Ferguson had been authorized to raise a force of 100 soldiers who would wear green uniforms, not the customary scarlet of the British Army. They would fight more like their very capable foe – the backwoodsmen among the rebels, who employed stealth, cover and camouflage, along with the deadly accuracy of the Kentucky long rifle.

The American officer, who was reported to have been in the company of a French hussar, was none other than General George Washington, commander of the Continental Army and future president of the United States. Ferguson stated that he actually had Washington in his sights twice that day, and even commanded the general to halt. 'On my calling, he stopped; but after looking at me proceeded,' continued the major. 'I again drew his attention, and made signs to him to stop, but he slowly continued on his way'.

During the Battle of Brandywine four days later, Ferguson's right elbow was shattered by a musket ball. After receiving treatment for his wound at a hospital on the battlefield, he wrote of his 7 September encounter. 'One of the surgeons who had been dressing the wounded rebel officers came in and told me that they had been informed that General Washington was all that day, with the light troops and only attended by a French officer in hussar dress, he himself dressed and mounted in every point as described'. Even then, Ferguson maintained, 'I am not sorry that I did not know at the time who it was'.

Although he never fully regained the use of his arm, Ferguson recovered to lead men in battle once again. On 7 October 1780, he was killed at the Battle of King's Mountain, by a rifle shot reported to have been fired from 411m (450 yards) away. His quest to raise an elite fighting force died with him. Had the chivalrous Ferguson shot Washington out of his saddle, the American Revolution might well have had a different outcome, and for that matter the history of the world.

By the time of the Revolution, the British Army was already acquainted with the 'irregular' combat tactics of backwoodsmen and Native Americans who had sided with their enemies. During the French and Indian War, an expedition led by General Edward Braddock against Fort Duquesne in western Pennsylvania met with disaster. On 13 July 1755, the British force of 2400 lost half its number killed and wounded when ambushed along the Monongahela River by a force of 900 French and Native American combatants. Braddock was killed in the engagement, and George Washington was also fortunate to escape with his life on this occasion.

ADVANCING TECHNOLOGY

The modern sniper may trace his lineage to the earliest days of the sighted firearm, but his evolution is rooted firmly in the era of wars for empire and conflict between Great Britain and her former colonies. Advancing technology was a key to the development of the sniper as well. The accuracy of the rifle was transforming the battlefield by the middle of the eighteenth century. This more accurate weapon would eventually take the place of the smoothbore musket.

The rifle itself came to prominence with game hunters in Central Europe and England in the seventeenth century, thence on to the New World. Its primary purpose, however, had remained as a hunting weapon. The use of the rifle in warfare had been discounted due to the expense of its manufacture and the time-consuming process required to load it. But, without regard for convention and the tactics of the European set-piece battle, American frontiersmen proved the rifle to indeed be a practical firearm which could be used to devastating effect in combat.

Born and raised in the wilderness and hunting game to survive, the colonial backwoodsman became as familiar with his small-calibre flintlock Kentucky rifle as he was with any other frontier necessity. On the day the American Revolution began, the colonial militia, known as minutemen for their ability to respond to an alarm at a moment's notice, harassed the British with accurate sharpshooting from concealed positions. Brigadier General Hugh Percy led a reinforcing column which came to the aid of the hard-pressed Redcoats retiring to Boston from Lexington and Concord.

Opposite: Clad in frontier buckskin, a member of Morgan's Riflemen demonstrates his prowess during target practice as members of other military units look on.

'As it began now to grow pretty late and we had [24km] 15 miles to retire, and only 36 rounds, I ordered the grenadiers and light infantry to move first; and covered them with my brigade sending out very strong flanking parties which were absolutely very necessary, as there was not a stone wall, or house, though before in appearance evacuated, from whence the rebels did not fire upon us', Percy wrote later. 'As soon as they saw us begin to retire, they pressed very much upon our rear guard, which for that reason, I relieved every now and then. In this manner, we retired for [24km] 15 miles under incessant fire all round us, till we arrived at Charlestown, between 7 and 8 in the evening and having expended almost all our ammunition'.

MORGAN'S RIFLEMEN

After the retreat from Concord, British forces were bottled up in Boston and continually under the watchful eyes of colonial marksmen. In his book *Firearms In American History*, Charles Winthrop Sawyer related, 'In the army around Boston the riflemen were employed as sharpshooters to pick off any British soldiers or officers who were incautious in exposing themselves. This they did to perfection.'

In June 1775, the Continental Congress endorsed the recruitment of 10 companies of sharpshooting backwoodsmen, recognizing the important role these units might play during the war for American independence. These soldiers dressed primarily in fringed buckskin and often carried knives or tomahawks as secondary weapons. One of the most famous regiments of sharpshooters was known as Morgan's Riflemen. Raised by Pennsylvania General Daniel Morgan, arguably the finest tactical field commander of the war and a cousin of pioneer legend Daniel Boone, the regiment, numbering 500, proved invaluable during the Saratoga campaign. One of their number, Tim Murphy, is remembered as the individual who felled Brigadier General Simon Fraser from a distance of 275 to 457m (300 to 500 yards) at the Battle of Bemis Heights on 7 October 1777.

While the smoke and fog of battle have caused accounts of the shot which killed Fraser to vary, Richard Brent, a Congressman from Virginia, related the incident as told to him by General Morgan himself 20 years later. Fraser, a Scot, showed 'all activity courage and vigilance, riding from one part of his division to another, and animating the troops by his example ... Morgan took a few of his best riflemen aside; men in whose fidelity, and fatal precision of aim, he could repose the most perfect confidence, and said to them: "that gallant officer is General Fraser; I admire and

CRACK SHOTS

In *Firearms In American History*, Charles Winthrop Sawyer charts the impressive feats of the American Colonists in the Revolutionary War:

'There is mention of a British soldier shot at [228m] 250 yards when only half his head was visible; of ten men, three of whom were officers, killed one day while reconnoitring; of a rifleman who, seeing some British on a scow at a distance of fully half a mile, found a good resting place on a hill and bombarded them until he potted the lot.'

respect him, but it is necessary that he should die – take your stations in that wood and do your duty." Within a few moments General Fraser fell, mortally wounded'.

In *Daniel Morgan, Revolutionary Rifleman*, author Don Higginbotham relates, 'At this point General Fraser, with the light infantry and the British 24th Regiment, attempted to form a line slightly to the rear of Riedesel's men to cover their movement. Mounted on a grey horse, Fraser rode back and forth shouting encouragement to his troops. Believing Fraser's efforts were prolonging the contest, Morgan called on rifleman Timothy Murphy to shoot the brave Scottish General. Murphy, a skilled Indian fighter and fine marksman, climbed a tree and trained his double-barrelled rifle upon Fraser. Allegedly his first shot severed the crupper of Fraser's horse, his second creased the horse's mane, and his third struck the General'.

Higginbotham recounts a British officer's version of a conversation he had with Morgan in late 1781. 'Me and my boys had a bad time until I saw that they were led by an officer on a grey horse – a devilish brave fellow,' Morgan commented. 'Then says I to one of my best shots, says I, you get up into that there tree, and single out him on the horse. Dang it, 'twas no sooner said than done. On came the British again, with the grey horseman leading; but his career was short enough this time. I jist tuck my eyes off him for a moment, and when I turned them to the place where he had been – pooh, he was gone!'

From his deathbed, Fraser was said to have told witnesses that he actually saw the rifleman who fired the fatal shot, aiming from a tree.

Captain Henry Beaufoy was among the handful of British officers who warned that a new day of warfare had dawned. His experience on the battlefield in the rebellious colonies led him to conclude that the rifleman must be acknowledged as the central figure in future wars. Indeed, during the coming conflict with Napoleonic France both sides would employ the rifle, in the hands of accomplished marksmen, to greater efficiency.

'The Americans, during their war with this country,' noted Beaufoy, 'were in the habit of forming themselves into small bands of ten or twelve, who, accustomed to shooting in hunting parties, went out in a sort of predatory warfare, each carrying his ammunition and provisions, and returning when they were exhausted. From the incessant attacks of these bodies, their opponents could never be prepared, as the first knowledge of a patrol in the neighbourhood was generally given by a volley of well-directed fire, that perhaps killed or wounded the greater part.'

Below: A soldier of the British 95th Rifles carries his Baker rifle at ease. During the Peninsular War (1808–14) against Napoleon, the three battalions of the 95th gained lasting fame.

RIFLEMEN OF THE NAPOLEONIC WARS

At the turn of the nineteenth century, the British Army did arm a single battalion of the 60th Foot with rifles. Then in 1802, the 95th Rifles, three battalions strong, were equipped with the recently adopted Baker rifle. As a member of the 95th during the Peninsular War, John Harris walked the field after the Battle of Vimeiro on 17 August 1808. He happened across a dead officer of the 50th Foot and determined that this man's shoes, for which he had no further use, might be a good fit.

'As I did so I was startled by the sharp report of a firelock, and, at the same moment, a bullet whistled close by my head. Instantly starting up, I turned, and looked in the direction from whence the shot had come. There was no person near me on this part of the field. The dead and the dying lay thickly all around; but nothing else I could see. I looked at the priming of my rifle, and again turned to the dead officer of the 50th. It was evident that some plundering scoundrel had taken a shot at me, and the fact of him doing so proclaimed him an enemy. To distinguish him amongst the bodies strewn about was impossible; perhaps he himself might be one of the wounded.

'Hardly had I effected the exchange, and put on the dead officer's shoes, and resumed my rifle, when another shot took place, and a second ball whistled past me. This time I was ready, and turning quickly, I saw my man: he was about to squat down behind a small mound. I took a haphazard shot at him, and instantly knocked him over. I immediately ran up to him; he had fallen on his face, and I heaved him over on his back, bestrode his body, and drew my sword bayonet. There was, however, no occasion for the precaution as he was even then in the agonies of death.

'It was a relief to me to find I had not been mistaken. He was a French light infantryman, and I therefore took it quite in the way of business – he had attempted my life, and lost his own. It was the fortune of war; so, stooping down, with my sword I cut the green string that sustained his calibash and took a hearty pull to quench my thirst.'

As the British army on the Iberian Peninsula retreated toward Corunna, Thomas Plunkett of the 1st Battalion, 95th Rifles, fired an astounding shot which killed the commander of the pursuing French force. On 3 January 1809, the 1st Battalion was serving as a rearguard, defending the approaches to a key bridge at the village of Cacabelos. At about 3 p.m., Plunkett spotted the Frenchman astride a handsome mount. In *Rifleman Thomas Plunkett: A Pattern for the Battalion*, Stuart Hadaway recounts the drama.

'The French commander, a dashing and talented young general called Auguste-Marie-Francois Colbert, seeing the rest of the 28th Foot and six guns of the Royal Horse Artillery formed up on the ridge on the far side of the Cua [river], withdrew his men to be reformed. Paget [British commander Sir Edward] also pulled his forces back, placing the 28th across the road on the far side with the 52nd and 95th formed up on either side in positions to pour flanking fire onto the bridge. It was this

'When Chipping fired, down he fell and in a minute we had his body with the horse in our possession behind the rock.'

Private Wheeler of the 95th Rifles on the death of a French cavalry officer at Waterloo

THE PERCUSSION CAP

One of the most important advances in the evolution of firearms was the development of the percussion cap, a small cap which fitted over a hollow tube leading into the firing chamber of a musket. Initially manufactured of steel and later copper, the percussion cap contained a mixture of fulminate of mercury and chloride of potash. When struck by the hammer, the mixture ignited, exploding the powder charge in the chamber and firing the weapon.

The stable but flammable mixture was patented by Reverend A.J. Forsyth in 1807. The cap was not developed for some time, however, and did not see widespread use for nearly three decades. When the percussion cap displaced the flintlock, it offered much greater reliability due to its closed system. The weapon was easier to operate in inclement weather than the open pan of the flintlock. Additionally the sniper was able to take aim without fear of an eyeful of burned powder when sighting.

BAKER RIFLE

Country of Origin	Great Britain
Calibre	17.88mm (0.7in)
Overall length	1012mm (44in)
Barrel length	760mm (30in)
Weight	4.1kg (9.03lb)

position that Colbert unwisely, and fatally, decided to assault. Forming his cavalry into a column of fours he charged for the bridge. Seeing Colbert charging ahead of his men, distinctive because of his uniform and grey horse, Plunkett raced ahead of the line and onto the bridge. Throwing himself onto his back and resting his Baker rifle on his crossed feet with the butt under his right shoulder in the approved manner, Plunkett fired at and killed Colbert. Apparently, having reloaded quickly, Plunkett then shot a second Frenchman who had ridden to Colbert's aid before dashing back to the British line.'

Estimates of the distance from which Plunkett's bullet found its mark vary, some purporting it to be as great as 730m (800 yards). Colbert was struck above the left eye and died within 15 minutes.

For more than two decades, Great Britain was at war with Napoleonic France. In 1951, historian B.H. Liddell-Hart edited the letters of a Private Wheeler, who served with the British Army from 1809 to 1828. A member of the 95th Rifles defending the farmhouse of La Haye Sainte during the climactic 1815 Battle of Waterloo, Wheeler wrote of being 'ordered with two men to post ourselves behind a rock or large stone, well studded with brambles.

'This was somewhat to our right and in advance. About an hour after we were posted we saw an officer of Huzzars sneaking down to get a peep at our position. One of my men was what we term a dead shot, when he was within point-blank distance. I asked him if he could make sure of him. His reply was "To be sure I can, but let him come nearer if he will, at all events his death warrant is signed and in my hands if he should turn back." By this time he had without perceiving us come up near to us. When Chipping fired, down he fell and in a minute we had his body with the horse in our possession behind the rock.'

The conquering army of Napoleon was the scourge of the European continent, achieving stunning victories from the Pyrenees to the Russian frontier. The French army corps were renowned for swift movement and rapid deployment on the battlefield. On 5 May 1807, an anonymous German observer penned a commentary on the tactics of Napoleon's fighting force.

'Each Marshall of the French Empire has a body of Two Thousand men of sharpshooters attached to his Corps d'armee,' noted the German. 'Such sharpshooters, all of which being expert and skilled men ... are always sure to hit their mark, at a distance of one hundred and fifty paces. In any cases, when the whole army is concentrating for a general battle, the several bodies of sharpshooters,

THE DEATH OF NELSON, 21 OCTOBER 1805

Napoleonic sharpshooting was not limited to land warfare. At the height of the Battle of Trafalgar, Admiral Horatio Nelson, the greatest naval commander in the history of the Royal Navy, strode the quarterdeck of his flagship, HMS *Victory*, locked in combat with the French *Redoutable*, which had sharpshooters posted in its rigging. Nelson was a conspicuous target, and he was hit by a musket ball at a reported range of less than 30m (100ft). The bullet struck the admiral in the shoulder and lodged in his spine.

Nelson lingered for several hours, long enough to hear that his victory over the Franco–Spanish fleet was total. The irony, however, that a great commander at the zenith of his career might be cut down by a single bullet while a major engagement swirled around him, resonates through history.

belonging to the Corps of each Marshall, are formed in one separate Corps by itself, consisting together of 16,000 men. Now, on whatever point, the Commander in Chief, is of intention ... to break through the opposing army, on such point or spot this select corps of 16,000 men is always sure to be placed and posted....

'As it is, this body of sharpshooters of 16,000 men may within a short time destroy double the quantity, say an opposing army of 30 to 40,000 men. Besides this select corps of sharpshooters, each Marshall commanding a body of Troops, has a certain number of skilled sharpshooters attached to each company of infantry, composing the Regiments that form such body of Troops. The purport entended [*sic*] by these shooters, consists exclusively to shoot dead the artillery men at the guns, as also such Officer, as stand afront the lines, but more particularly to aim at the Chief Commander of the opponents, being always sure to hit their mark at a distance of 150 Military paces ...'

THE WAR OF 1812

Below: British soldiers labour to improve their positions at Sevastopol during the Crimean War, while a victim of deadly accurate sniper fire is attended to (far right).

During the period of the Napoleonic Wars, a conflict between Great Britain and her former colonies in America erupted. In 1814, the British 3rd Brigade marched on Washington D.C., the capital city of the young United States. Eventually, these troops put the city and the Executive Mansion (later to become the White House), the residence of President James Madison, to the torch. On their approach to Washington, the British were met with sniper fire from a house along the route of march. One soldier was killed, and the commanding general's horse was shot.

Both sides employed regiments of sharpshooters during the War of 1812. At the climactic Battle of New Orleans, the British marched directly into concentrated American rifle fire and suffered heavy casualties. In *Green Coats and Glory*, Dr John C. Fredriksen concluded, 'The Regiment of Rifles was unquestionably the most effective infantry formation fielded by the United States in the War of 1812 ... Accurate weapons, a soaring *esprit de corps* and inspired leadership ... all resulted in consistently superior performance.... At Conjocta Creek, the skill in planning and the firmness in the execution by the riflemen defeated the designs of the British and saved the entire American army.'

RIFLED MUSKETS

The momentum of the Industrial Revolution allowed factories to produce rifled muskets, fired via the percussion lock rather than flintlock ignition of the powder charge, in significant quantities by the middle of the nineteenth century. In the hands of a skilled marksman, this new generation of weapon was up to 10 times more accurate than the smoothbore musket. Consequently, the footsoldier had become a much more lethal instrument of war.

In 1848, the introduction of the cone-shaped Minié ammunition offered greater accuracy for rifles than the former spherical ball. The 'Minié ball' was faster to load, and when fired it expanded to fill the entire barrel, catching the rifling quickly and increasing muzzle velocity. By the mid-1850s, the British Army adopted the muzzle-loading Enfield rifle, which offered the potential for more accurate long-range shooting, but few of these reached the troops fighting in the distant Crimea or during the insurrection in India, who were still equipped with the Minié. More than half a century before the stagnation and trench warfare of the Western Front in World War I, the opposing British and Russian forces experienced an eerily similar situation during the Crimean War of 1853–56. Lieutenant Colonel David Davidson of the 1st City of Edinburgh Rifle Volunteers developed a basic telescopic rifle sight after witnessing a team of sharpshooters in action at the siege of Sevastopol.

FIRST TELESCOPIC SIGHT

During the siege of Sevastopol, Lieutenant Colonel David Davidson of the 1st City of Edinburgh Rifle Volunteers recalled:

'One soldier was observed lying with his rifle carefully pointed at a distant embrasure and with his finger on the trigger ready to pull, while by his side lay another with a telescope directed at the same object. He, with the telescope, was anxiously watching the moment when a gunner should show himself, in order that he might give the signal to fire.'

THE AMERICAN CIVIL WAR

From 1861 to 1865, the world witnessed the ascendancy of the rifle as an instrument of precision killing on a grand scale. When political turmoil in America boiled over into civil war, the rifled musket was standard issue. The conflict between the Union of Northern states and the Southern Confederacy became a proving ground for the

17

'BOB THE NAILER'

At roughly the same time as the Crimean War, the ability of the British to maintain order in their far-flung empire was tested by a rebellion in India. With the exception of the Residency, the entire city of Lucknow in northern India had fallen to the so-called Sepoys. The garrison of the Residency endured a protracted siege, during which they learned first-hand of the prowess of the Sepoy sharpshooters. The deadliest of these harassed the British at every opportunity. Accounts of the siege vary slightly as to the grudgingly respectful nickname he was given. However, both 'Jim the Nailer' and 'Bob the Nailer' convey the point.

Bob the Nailer was reputed to be an African who had served in the army of the King of Oudh, who actually did fire iron nails from his musket. In order to silence him, the British were forced to dig a tunnel and detonate an explosive charge to destroy the house in which he was located.

Another account relates, 'The only way fire could be returned was from concealment. The garrison came gradually to encourage the assailants to occupy a point and to have confidence in occupying it. But they marked well the direction; and during the night they bored holes in that direction. In the morning the enemy would come up by twos and threes to occupy their chosen post. Then the muskets would be discharged. The result was almost inevitably successful.

'But there was a wily marksman whom this guileful device entirely failed to snare. Choosing his coign with infinite subtlety and care, he would await the appearance of a likely target with an unblinking watchfulness that dawn-chill or the heat of the noonday sun in no way seemed to affect. Unseen, undetectable, he would remain inactive for hours at a stretch. But if a gleam of scarlet tunic or white cap cover came to reward his vigil, then his swift, unerring shot took toll with a deadly precision that scorned the waste of a single cartridge.

'In wry tribute to his outstanding skill, the sweating men of the garrison dubbed him "Jim the Nailer". To give the exact tally of his score against the Residency's garrison is as impossible as to cloak him with a specific identity or pronounce upon his ultimate fate. For with the relief of Lucknow, no more was heard of him.'

breech-loading rifle and the tactics of the stealthy sniper, armed with weapons which could kill at greater distances than ever before.

For 15 years prior to the outbreak of the Civil War, Hiram Berdan had been acknowledged as one of the best marksmen in the United States. Berdan, a mechanical engineer who had invented a repeating rifle and a specialized type of ammunition before the war, complemented this talent with an energetic drive for self-promotion. When war came, he raised two regiments, totalling nearly 2000 soldiers, which came to be known collectively as Berdan's Sharpshooters.

Quickly, these hand-picked riflemen captured the imagination of the public – and not without reason. Before he was accepted as a member of the elite force, each individual was required to pass a rigorous qualification test. It was necessary for the soldier to place 10 consecutive shots within a target only 25.4cm (10in) in diameter from 183m (200 yards). Berdan's Sharpshooters used the Sharp's 13.2mm (0.52in) calibre breech-loading rifle. This model fired a cartridge which included the bullet and a sack of paper or thin cloth, which contained the powder charge. Target rifles equipped with telescopic sights were also used at various times.

The Sharpshooters were uniformed to stand out among the rest of the Union Army of the Potomac but to blend in with woodland foliage for optimum concealment. While the rest of the army wore standard-issue blue uniforms, Berdan's men were clothed in forest-green wool frock coats and trousers. Their green forage caps were often adorned with black ostrich feathers, and their buttons were made of black rubber rather than brass. They wore brogan shoes and knee-length leather gaiters to protect against the brambles and briars of the wilderness.

During the siege of Yorktown, Virginia, in the spring of 1862, one of Berdan's men, a New Hampshire soldier remembered only as 'Old Seth', was observed to have accomplished quite a feat. Finding an empty rifle pit previously dug by Confederates, he slipped into it early one morning. In this vantage point near the rebel lines, he reportedly remained for two straight days, resupplied with food and ammunition by his comrades. During that time, he systematically shot gunner after gunner, rendering an artillery piece untenable.

Below: A Confederate skirmisher dispatches a Union soldier whose misfortune it was to be assigned to picket duty. Due to shortages, the competition for the best rifles was keen among rebel soldiers.

Berdan's two regiments of keen-eyed riflemen included a number of characters. One of these, a member of Company C of the 1st Regiment, was Truman Head, known to his comrades as 'California Joe'. The record of this legendary figure's life is somewhat sketchy and contradictory, but he is believed to have been born in Philadelphia and travelled west as a gold prospector and hunter. The story goes that he enlisted in the fall of 1861 and that his exploits as a sharpshooter were soon publicized in newspapers across the Union. One of these published an account that he had 'shot a man out of a tree two miles off, just at daybreak, first pop'. California Joe had invested in his own Sharp's rifle before the weapon's use was widespread in the Federal army. He was considerably older than most soldiers, with estimates of his age at enlistment ranging from 42 to 52 years. Obviously, he had lied in order to join up, and eventually he was discharged for health reasons.

CONFEDERATE SHARPSHOOTERS

Berdan himself did not see the end of the war in uniform. Although he had led Union brigades at Chancellorsville and Gettysburg, his claims of his own battlefield prowess were considered by many to be exaggerated. He was described by one individual as 'most unscrupulous and totally unfit for command'. He resigned from the Federal army early in 1864 and died in 1893 at the age of 68.

The Confederate armies employed sharpshooters generally among their ranks rather than concentrating them in specific units. These soldiers were used as skirmishers and often allowed to operate independently, seeking targets of opportunity and harassing the enemy. The most prized rifles were those which were smuggled through the Union blockade of Southern ports and imported from England. Chief among these firearms were those manufactured by the Whitworth

Right: *This sketch shows Union general John F. Reynolds reeling on his horse, having been hit by a Confederate marksman at the Battle of Gettysburg. Reynolds led his I Corps from the front and paid for the decision with his life.*

WHITWORTH RIFLE

Country of Origin	Great Britain
Calibre	11.43mm (0.45in)
Overall length	1250mm (49in)
Barrel length	760mm (30in)
Weight	4.05kg (9lb)

and Kerr companies, most of which were capable of incorporating a telescopic sight. Since these rifles were relatively scarce, competition was keen among rebel soldiers for the privilege of carrying such weapons and operating as a sharpshooter.

While Berdan's troops had the upper hand early in the siege of Yorktown, the situation slowly began to change. In *To the Gates of Richmond, The Peninsular Campaign*, author Stephen W. Sears noted, "'Our Sharp Shooters play mischief with them when they come out in daylight,' one of Berdan's men told his wife.

'A rough balance was restored with the arrival at Yorktown of John Bell Hood's Texas brigade from [Joseph E.] Johnston's army. Hood's men had a sizeable number of British-made Enfield rifles and knew how to use them. When the Yankee sharpshooters grew too bold, the Texans would slip into the forward picket line for what they liked to call a little squirrel shooting. Soon their fire would drive the Federals out of the trees and other hiding places they favoured and back into their fortifications, where sharpshooting continued but on more even terms. The marksmen on both sides at Yorktown considerably exaggerated their prowess, especially to credulous newspaper correspondents, yet there was no doubt that because of them the prudent learned to keep their heads down. The story quickly got around, for example, of the Confederate soldier who woke up one morning in his cramped trench and unthinkingly stood up to stretch and was instantly shot through the heart.'

Indeed, the Confederates utilized a deadly combination of stealth, camouflage and the superior Whitworth rifle. An illustration of the value placed on the British-made weapon is the fact that Private John West, a Georgian, was one of only 13 soldiers so equipped in the entire Confederate Army of Northern Virginia.

West remembered, 'We frequently resorted to various artifices in our warfare. Sometimes we would climb a tree and pin leaves all over our clothes to keep their colour from betraying us. When two of us would be together and a Yankee sharpshooter would be trying to get a shot at us, one of us would put his hat on a ramrod and poke it up from behind the object that concealed and protected us, and when the Yankee showed his head to shoot at the hat the other one would put a bullet through his head. I have shot them out of trees and seen them fall like 'coons. When we were in grass or grain we would fire and fall over and roll … from the spot whence we fired and the Yankee sharpshooters would fire away at the smoke.'

In May 1863 at Chancellorsville, General Robert E. Lee and his chief lieutenant, General Thomas J. 'Stonewall' Jackson, fought the tactical masterpiece battle of the Civil War. Lee divided his army, holding a line before General Joseph Hooker's numerically superior Army of the Potomac. Jackson and a substantial rebel force marched along a concealed route and fell upon the Union XI Corps at the extreme right flank of the Yankee line. Hooker's army was routed. On the evening of his greatest triumph and at the zenith of his career, Jackson was mortally wounded by friendly fire.

WORTH A REGIMENT

Confederate army Private John West recalled: 'Artillerymen could stand anything better than they could sharpshooting, and they would turn their guns upon a sharpshooter as quick as they would upon a battery. You see, we could pick off the gunners so easily. Myself and a comrade completely silenced a battery of six guns in less than two hours on one occasion. The battery was then stormed and captured. I heard General [Robert E.] Lee say he would rather have those 13 sharpshooters than any regiment in the army.'

BERDAN'S SHARPSHOOTERS

Jackson, however, was not the only general officer to die at Chancellorsville. The sharpshooters were on the field as well. In *Chancellorsville 1863: The Souls Of The Brave*, Ernest B. Furgurson recounts, 'Near Chandler's house, at the apex of Hooker's line above Chancellorsville, Union general Amiel Whipple sat on his horse in the morning sun, watching his men improve their breastworks. A Rebel sniper in a tree nearby was annoying them. Whipple started to scratch out an order for some of Berdan's Sharpshooters to rid them of this nuisance. *Thunk*. The Confederate rifleman's next round struck Whipple's belt in front and came out the back between his coat buttons, mortally wounding him. One of Berdan's lieutenants crept past the Union skirmishers, watching for the sniper, and potted him before he could fire again. He brought back a rifle, a fox-skin cap, $1600 in Confederate money, and $100 in US paper.'

The two regiments of Berdan's Sharpshooters operated in tandem at Chancellorsville, serving as the spearhead for an attack against the trailing elements of Jackson's wagon train during the flanking march. One regiment pinned the Confederate 23rd Georgia down in the cut of an unfinished railroad, while the other outflanked the position. While only three rebels were killed in the engagement, 296 laid down their arms and marched into captivity rather than risk showing themselves to return fire and becoming targets for the sharp-eyed Federals. Union Lieutenant George Marden wrote later, 'It was a most splendid affair and the praise of the Sharpshooters was in everybody's mouth.'

The epic Battle of Gettysburg ended Robert E. Lee's second invasion of the North and the possibility of a major Confederate victory on Northern soil. The Army of the Potomac, now under General George Meade, held the high ground from Culp's Hill and Cemetery Hill on the right, across Cemetery Ridge to the anchor of Little Round Top on the extreme left. On successive days, 1–3 July 1863, Lee's troops unsuccessfully assaulted the Union positions and were forced to retire into Virginia.

One of the most famous photographs of the Civil War was taken on the field at Gettysburg. A jumble of huge boulders known as Devil's Den was the scene of heavy fighting on 2 July. When rebel soldiers wrested control of the area from its defenders, Devil's Den became an ideal location for sharpshooters who picked off Union soldiers along the crest of Little Round Top. The photo, which was probably posed, was alleged to depict a dead Confederate sharpshooter, killed by a shell fragment in his sniper's nest. The rifle in the photo is not a weapon which appears to have been used by a sharpshooter, and the same body is used in other scenes captured by photographers Alexander Gardner and Timothy O'Sullivan, who reached the Gettysburg area with their travelling darkroom before the dead were buried.

During the crucial opening hours at Gettysburg, the commander of the Union left wing, General John F. Reynolds, was encouraging the men of the 2nd Wisconsin

Above: *From a concealed position high in a tree, his rifle balanced on a branch, a Union sharpshooter surveys the approaches for unwary rebels who might cross his path.*

FAMOUS LAST WORDS

At the Battle of Spotsylvania on 9 May 1864, General John Sedgwick, commander of the Union VI Corps, was supervising the disposition of some artillery batteries along the front line. Continuous and accurate fire from Confederate sharpshooters had made the soldiers near Sedgwick skittish.

Theodore Lyman, an aide to General Meade, described what happened next. '[H]e noticed a soldier dodging the bullets as they came over. Rising from the grass, he went up to the man, and, laying his hand on his shoulder, said, "Why, what are you dodging for? They could not hit an elephant at that distance." As he spoke the last word, he fell, shot through the brain by a ball from a telescopic rifle.'

One report said that the shot that killed Sedgwick was fired from a Whitworth rifle at 730m (800 yards).

Regiment as they moved forward. Astride a large black horse, Reynolds was a tempting target. 'Forward men, forward for God's sake, and drive those fellows out of the woods,' Reynolds exhorted. A moment later, the general glanced toward the observation post in the tower of a nearby Lutheran seminary. Suddenly, he reeled in the saddle, struck by a bullet behind his right ear.

In *Gettysburg – The First Day*, Harry Pfanz relates the memory of Private Charles Veil, Reynolds' orderly. 'Veil vaulted from his horse and ran to Reynolds, who was lying on his left side and had a bruise above his left eye. Veil thought that he was stunned. He grasped the general under the arms; Capts. Robert W. Mitchell and Edward C. Baird joined him. Each took a leg, and they carried the general from the perils of the woods.... They did not realize that their general was dead, but they surely knew he was out of the fight.... They carried his body on a stretcher to the George house on the Emmitsburg Road. There Veil remembered seeing the general's wound for the first time; he recalled it as a small hole at the base of his skull that did not bleed.'

In July 1864, a Confederate force under General Jubal Early conducted raids in Northern territory, burning the town of Chambersburg, Pennsylvania, and threatening Washington D.C. President Abraham Lincoln, in company with his wife, Mary Todd Lincoln, ventured out to Fort Stevens on the capital city's defensive perimeter. Early's Confederates could see the dome of the Capitol building, but they were not strong enough to attack in force.

Lincoln climbed atop the parapet and scanned the horizon. His secretary, John Hay, recorded the events of 11–12 July in his diary. 'The President concluded to ... travel around the defenses.... At three o'clock P.M. the President came in bringing the news that the enemy's advance was at Ft. Stevens on the 7th Street road. He was in the Fort when it was first attacked, standing upon the parapet. A soldier roughly ordered him to get down or he would have his head knocked off [12 July 1864]…. The President again made the tour of the fortifications; was again under fire at Ft. Stevens; a man was shot at his side …'

The soldier to which Hay referred was very likely future US Supreme Court Justice Oliver Wendell Holmes Jr. Without knowing who the careless civilian was, Holmes barked, 'Get down, you damn fool, before you get shot.' Lincoln was said to have agreed to sit behind the parapet, but to the distress of his entourage, he continued to stand up repeatedly to get a better view. Holmes' advice was certainly sound; the sharpshooter's bullet made no distinction in terms of rank or station.

THE BREECH-LOADER

During the latter part of the nineteenth century, the muzzle-loading rifle was gradually replaced by a succession of improving breech-loading and lever-action rifles. A faster rate of fire and cheaper production costs made the demise of the muzzle-loader as a front-line infantry weapon inevitable. The lever-action 11.1mm

Below: Shot by a Confederate sniper at Spotsylvania, Union General John Sedgwick lies dead, mourned by his staff. Seconds after a fateful rebuke to a soldier, the general was killed from an estimated distance of 730m (800 yards).

Above: *This painting from 1839 depicts British India's dangerous and disputed Northwest Frontier. Baluchi snipers, hidden behind a massive rock wall, wait for the opportune moment to open fire on a Sepoy column, not realizing that they are about to be fired upon themselves.*

(0.44in) calibre Winchester became a legendary weapon of the American West, while the armies of Europe preferred single-shot breech-loading models such as the 11.4mm (0.45in) calibre Martini-Henry, which was issued to British soldiers beginning in 1871. That same year, German manufacturer Mauser introduced its Model 1871, which was followed by an improved version, firing a 7.92mm (0.31in) bullet 17 years later.

Scientists, including Alfred Nobel, worked throughout the nineteenth century to improve on the black powder which had been used as a firearm propellant for years without modification. By the 1880s, a more powerful and virtually smokeless powder was introduced in rifle cartridges. The sniper of conflicts to come would owe much of his success to the improved concealment afforded by this invention.

In *Sniper*, author Adrian Gilbert noted this considerable advantage. 'The new propellants also made the "smoke of battle" a thing of the past; soldiers were no longer enveloped in clouds of white smoke once the shooting began. Previously, a single shot marked the sniper's position; now only the muzzle flash was visible, and a well-concealed sniper could normally hide the flash. This factor alone gave the sniper an enormous advantage: he was able to roam the battlefield as a near invisible assassin, producing a terrorizing effect on the morale of enemy troops.'

SHARPSHOOTERS IN THE BOER WAR

The discovery of gold in the state of Transvaal was the spark which indirectly ignited the Second Boer War of 1899–1901. Sporadic violence had plagued the region since Britain acquired territory in southern Africa during the Napoleonic Wars. Years of bad blood between the Boer farmers of Dutch descent, who occupied Transvaal and the Orange Free State, and the British subjects who populated the area to the south toward Cape Town and the colony of Natal to the east erupted in armed conflict. The Boer War became a proving ground for recent improvements in small arms.

The Boers soon asserted themselves as superior marksmen and masters of non-traditional tactics. They were farmers who lived their lives on the *veldt*, hunting game to supplement their crops. Using their magazine-fed Mauser rifles, the Boers inflicted heavy casualties on British troops, often at such distances that return fire was impossible. The Boers also made use of camouflage, their clothing blending into the native vegetation, beards on their faces, and slouch hats pulled low over their foreheads. Eventually, the weight of British military superiority brought the Boers to heel, after the nation's military establishment had learned an expensive lesson.

The most celebrated Boer guerrilla leader, Christiaan de Wet, distracted British troops during more than one lengthy campaign. A history of one of these operations describes the capabilities of the Boer riflemen. 'On each side of the line were ditches, and at dawn on the seventh day of the investment, it was found that these had been occupied by snipers during the night, and that it was impossible to water the animals.... About noon several companies of Scots and Welsh Fusiliers advanced from different directions in very extended order upon the ditches. Captain Baillie's company of the former regiment first attracted the fire of the burghers [Boers]. Wounded twice the brave officer staggered on until a third bullet struck him dead. Six of his men were found lying beside him.'

By the dawn of the twentieth century, some tacticians grudgingly acknowledged that they would be required to reckon with the sniper on future battlefields. In the coming years, the art of the sniper would reach new levels of refinement.

Below: *Armed with German Mauser rifles and ammunition clips and wearing their trademark slouch hats, Boer sharpshooters, hardened by war, pose for a rare photograph.*

From a shallow trench on the Western Front, a British soldier searches for a target while his companion waves a helmet hung across a shovel to attract fire from the German lines. Such tactics were used to draw enemy fire, allowing the rifleman to locate the source and so return fire, possibly silencing a deadly enemy sniper.

CHAPTER TWO

TRENCH WARFARE

During World War I, the static hell of trench warfare claimed millions of lives across Europe. In sharp contrast to long hours of monotony, death might come in a flash at the hand of the sniper, unseen and unheard until the final moment.

The crack of the sniper's rifle ends the life of Paul Baumer amid the squalor of the trenches. 'He fell in October 1918, on a day that was so quiet and still on the whole front, that the army report confined itself to the single sentence: All quiet on the Western Front,' wrote Erich Maria Remarque of his fictional German soldier in his book of the same title. The author offers no additional details of how Baumer dies, but filmmakers have chosen the solitary bullet. Remarque himself had been wounded five times in combat during World War I, and while Baumer's demise is intensely personal for the reader, his was an end played out over and over during the Great War of 1914–18.

When the land forces of the Allies and the Central Powers failed to reach a swift and conclusive end to the war on the battlefield, the conflict on the Western Front lapsed into one of attrition. Opposing armies faced one another from trench lines stretching from the North Sea to the Swiss frontier. Between them lay a barren, shell-pocked killing ground called No Man's Land. The stagnant war in the trenches of Flanders and France meant cruel hardship for soldiers on both sides. The stench of death hung in the air. Thick, oozing mud and vermin were constant companions.

Into this sometimes surreal existence stepped a stealthy rifleman, whose mission was to exact his toll with the well-placed single shot, to gather intelligence, and to demoralize the enemy as much as possible. Without a shadow of a doubt, along with the continuous dread of death-dealing artillery fire and poisonous gas, the spectre of the sniper preyed on the infantryman's psyche.

On the eve of the Great War, the British Army was considered by many to be the finest in the world when participating in combat which favoured massed troops delivering heavy, sustained fire in a relatively concentrated area. This conflict, however, degenerated into a different kind of war. The primary British rifle was the 0.303in (7.7mm) Short

GEWEHR 98

Country of Origin	Germany
Calibre	7.92mm (0.31in)
Overall length	1250mm (49.2in)
Barrel length	740mm (29.1in)
Weight	3.9kg (8.6lb)

Magazine Lee-Enfield (SMLE). This model was augmented by a variety of hunting rifles, and many snipers later opted to utilize the longer Rifle No. 3 Mk I, which was more commonly referred to as the P14 and was American-made. Early telescopic sights were attached to the SMLE offset to the side, complicating the ability of the shooter to fix a target. Canadian snipers often used the Ross rifle, which was manufactured in their own country.

GERMAN ADVANTAGE

Although the French Army also included some designated snipers, the initial advantage in sniping lay decidedly with the Germans. Excellent marksmen, many of whom had hunted for years or served as gamekeepers on the large estates of their country's aristocracy, were stationed down to the company level in the German Army. A battalion sniper section included up to 24 men. These specialists were generally armed with the sharpshooter's rifle, the fine 7.92mm (0.31in) *Scharfschützen Gewehr* 98, a later version of the proven Mauser bolt-action design. Germany had long been recognized as a producer of outstanding optical instruments, and the snipers were supplied with telescopic sights, usually factory-fitted to their rifles and of three-power or better. The British, on the other hand, could muster relatively few suitable optical instruments, and an appeal to the populace resulted in the donation of thousands of pairs of binoculars. When the United States entered the war in April 1917, some soldiers were armed with Springfield Model 1903 rifles enhanced with telescopic sights.

In preparing their trenches, the Germans made use of irregular lines, daubed their sandbags with paint for concealment, and endeavoured to make themselves less conspicuous to enemy snipers. The British were slower to adapt, digging their trenches initially in straighter lines. Over time, both sides also made great use of discarded sheet metal, piles of bricks, broken glass or any other material which might make their trenches more difficult to discern.

During the first two years of the war, German pre-eminence in the art of sniping resulted in their virtual domination of No Man's Land. A typical day in the Allied trenches might find a single battalion losing up to 18 men to sniper fire. Herbert McBride, an American who fought with Canadian troops, was credited with more than 100 kills as a sniper. He respected the ability of the German adversary, who was particularly deadly from the relatively close range of the opposing trenches, often less than 182m (200 yards).

Of the enemy's bullet, McBride wrote, 'At short ranges, due to the high velocity, it does have an explosive effect and, not only the effect but, when it strikes, it sounds like an explosion ... all of a sudden, you hear a "whop" and the man alongside goes down. If it is daylight and you are looking that way, you may see a little tuft sticking out from his clothes. Wherever the bullet comes out it carries a little of the clothing ... the sound of a bullet hitting a man can never be mistaken for anything else ... the effect of the bullet, at short range, also suggests the idea of an explosion, especially if a large bone be struck. I remember one instance where one of our men was struck in the knee and the bullet almost amputated the leg. He died before he could be taken to the dressing station.'

Below: Near the half-buried body of a French soldier, a German sniper rises cautiously to survey No Man's Land. On the Western Front, the hunter often became the hunted.

After the war, McBride penned a chronicle of his trench fighting experiences. *A Rifleman Went To War* provides glimpses of sniper tactics and fieldcraft. Its practical application was still valid half a century later when US Marine instructors utilized it as an aid in training snipers for the jungles and rice paddies of Vietnam.

Major Hesketh Vernon Hesketh-Prichard had been a writer, champion cricketer and renowned big game hunter before the war. At the age of 38, his application for military service was declined at first. Later, he was able to make his way to the front as an escort for war correspondents. Hesketh-Prichard soon realized that the disparity in sniper skills had to be addressed. In his 1920 book *Sniping In France*, he described the situation he found.

'At this time the skill of the German sniper had become a byword, and in the early days of trench warfare brave German riflemen used to lie between the lines, sending their bullets through the head of any officer or man who dared to look over our parapet. These Germans, who were often forest guards, and sometimes battle police, did their business with a skill and a gallantry which must be freely acknowledged. From the ruined house or the field of decaying roots, sometimes resting their rifles on the bodies of the dead, they sent forth a plague of head-shot wounds into the British line. Their marks were small, but when they hit they usually killed their man, and the hardiest soldier turned sick when he saw the effect of the pointed German bullet, which was apt to keyhole so that the little hole in the forehead where it entered often became a huge tear, the size of a man's fist, on the other side of the stricken man's head.'

In a letter to his father dated 26 February 1915, Alan Seeger, a young American soldier serving with Commonwealth troops, recounted a brush with death that was all too familiar to his comrades.

'I was shot a few days ago coming in from sentinel duty. I exposed myself for about two seconds at a point where the communication ditch is not deep enough. One of the snipers who keep cracking away with their Mausers at any one who shows his head came within an ace of getting me. The ball just grazed my arm, tore the sleeve of my capote and raised a lump on the biceps which is still sore, but the skin was not broken and the wound was not serious enough to make me leave the ranks.'

'The Germans are marvellous [*sic*],' Seeger continued. 'You hear their rifles only a few hundred metres off, you feel them about you all the time, and yet you can never see them. Only last night when the moon set behind the crest, it silhouetted the heads of two sentinels in their big trench on top.'

TRENCH SONG

Out of grudging respect, the German sniper was lauded in the songs sung in the trenches as well. One example ran:

The turret towers that stood in the air,
Sheltered a foeman sniper there –
They found, who fell to the sniper's aim,
A field of death on the field of fame;
And stiff in khaki the boys were laid
To the sniper's toll at the barricade,
But the quick went clattering through the town,
Shot at the sniper and brought him down,
As we entered Loos in the morning.

LEE-ENFIELD SMLE

Country of Origin	Great Britain
Calibre	0.303in (7.7mm)
Overall length	1129mm (44.4in)
Barrel length	640mm (25.2in)
Weight	4.14kg (9.12lb)

Hesketh-Prichard battled not only the Germans but the rigidity of the British high command as well. He was eventually named sniping officer of the 4th Division and in 1915 established the First Army Sniping, Observation and Scouting (SOS) School near the French town of Bethune. A 17-day course of study included the care and maintenance of the rifle, proper sighting, the use of camouflage, and map reading. Soon, a second school began operating. That same year, formal battalion sniper organizations emerged in the British Army. These included 16 trained riflemen and at least two noncommissioned officers.

BRITISH SNIPER CORPS

The trainees were taught to work in pairs, switching the roles of sniper and observer periodically to maximize effectiveness, since fatigue could easily set in after a short period of viewing enemy trenches through magnification. The perilous prospect of scanning the enemy's positions for potential targets could quickly turn the hunter into the hunted, and both sides utilized viewing periscopes and telescopes to search the horizon. On more than one occasion, a glint of reflected sunlight caused these periscopes to become targets themselves.

The Lovat Scouts, a 200-man unit whose ranks consisted of many experienced Scottish hunters and game wardens, or 'ghillies', directed much of the initial training of the fledgling British sniper corps. Pioneers of modern fieldcraft, the Lovat Scouts emphasized the elements of stealth, of which camouflage was an important component. They introduced the ghillie suit, the combination of a long robe, a hood or veil, and attached concealing vegetation, which they had employed on highland estates to stalk game and arrest poachers. Major F.M. Crum also made a significant contribution to early British sniper training.

Snipers on both sides sometimes constructed nests of heavy steel plates with firing loopholes cut into them facing the enemy and a curtain suspended at the rear of the position to prevent a telltale shaft of light from streaking through. Elaborate camouflage such as fake trees, dummy corpses, or even burlap or canvas sewn together to resemble a dead horse might harbour a hidden sniper. The most effective snipers worked from multiple positions, changing location periodically.

Snipers became masters of the practice of deception, hoping to draw fire by creating dummy loopholes, showing helmets or caps on poles above parapets, and employing dummy heads made of *papier maché*. From a distance, these heads looked lifelike, and more enterprising soldiers even lit cigarettes and smoked them through tubes from the safety of cover below. Paths to water sources, latrines and shallow communications trenches became favourite haunts of the sniper.

The nature of the sniper's participation in war made him something of a loner, a breed apart even among his fellow soldiers. While those, both Allied and German, who had hunted game before the war often became the most proficient at hunting men on the battlefield, others could only make the transition to human quarry with great difficulty. Still others could not make it at all.

Below: *Emerging cautiously from the concealment of a drainage pipe, a trio of Belgian sharpshooters with fixed bayonets prepare for action with German scouts.*

LIGHTING UP

One of only 13 infantry officers to receive the *Pour le Mérite*, the highest German award for valour, (commonly known as the 'Blue Max'), during World War I, Ernst Junger served with the 73rd Hanoverian Fusilier Regiment. Between the world wars, he became an author of eminent status, and in *Copse 125* he related a hunt for enemy soldiers who had been firing at German positions. Accompanied by his spotter, H., Junger crept into No Man's Land.

'Suddenly a sound rang out – a sound foreign to this noontide scene, an ominous clinking as of a helmet or a bayonet striking the side of a trench. At the same moment I felt a hand grip my leg and heard a low-breathed whistle behind me. It was H., for he had passed those hours in the same alert attention as I.'

'I pushed back with my foot to warn him,' Junger continued, 'and at the same moment a greenish-yellow shadow flitted across the exposed part of the trench. It was a tall figure in clay-coloured uniform, with a flat helmet set well down over his forehead and both hands grasping his rifle, which was slung from his neck by a strap. It must have been the relief as he came from the rear; and now it could only be a matter of seconds till the man he relieved passed across the same spot. I sighted my rifle on it sharply.

'A murmuring of voices arose from behind the screen of grass, broken now and again by suppressed laughter or a soft clanking. Then a tiny puff of smoke ascended – the moment had come when the returning post lit a pipe or cigarette for the way back. And in fact he appeared a moment later, first his helmet only, next his whole figure. His luck was against him, for just as he came in line of aim, he turned round and took his cigarette from his mouth – probably to add a word that occurred to him during the few steps he had come. It was his last, for at that moment the iron chain between shoulder, hand and butt was drawn tight and the patch pocket on the left side of his tunic was taken as clearly on the foresight as though it were on the very muzzle of the rifle. Thus the shot took the words from his mouth. I saw him fall, and having seen many fall before this, I knew he would never get up again. He fell first against the side of the trench and then collapsed into a heap that obeyed the force of life no longer but only the force of gravity.'

A BREED APART

Writing of his first experience on sniper duty in the autumn of 1915, R.A. Chell noted, 'After about 15 minutes quiet watching – with my rifle in a ready position – I saw a capless bald head come up behind the plate. The day was bright and clear and I hadn't the slightest difficulty in taking a most deliberate aim at the very centre of that bright and shiny plate – but somehow I couldn't press the trigger: to shoot such a "sitter" so deliberately in cold blood required more real courage than I possessed. After a good look round he went down and I argued with myself about my duty. My bald-headed opponent had been given a very sporting chance and if he were fool enough to come up again I must shoot him unflinchingly. I considered it my duty to be absolutely ready for that contingency. After about two minutes he

'Sniper Sandy's
slaying Saxon
soldiers,
And Saxon
soldiers seldom
show but Sandy
slays a few,
And every day the
Boches put up
little wooden
crosses,
In the cemetery
for Saxon soldiers
sniper Sandy
slew.'

Song dedicated to
Sergeant Sandy
MacDonald

came up again with added boldness and I did my duty. I had been a marksman before the war and so had no doubt about the instantaneousness of that man's death. I felt funny for days and the shooting of another German at "stand-to" the next morning did nothing to remove those horrid feelings I had.'

As the gap in sniping proficiency closed, Allied shooters began exacting some measure of revenge. Counter-sniper operations and duels between rival merchants of death became more commonplace. Sergeant Sandy MacDonald, a highland gamekeeper in peacetime, had a reputation for accuracy up to 914m (1000 yards). As a member of the 5th Battalion, Seaforths, he was credited with 97 confirmed kills before losing his own life in action at Beaumont Hamel in 1917. His exploits were celebrated in a short verse (see sidebar).

Out of necessity, the sniper operated in seclusion. His feats of marksmanship, courage and stealth were often unseen and therefore went without praise. The London Gazette printed the citation of the only sniper who was awarded the Victoria Cross during World War I. The Commonwealth's highest decoration for valour in combat was awarded posthumously to Private Thomas Barratt, 7th Battalion, South Staffordshire Regiment, who was killed on 27 July 1917, near Ypres.

'For most conspicuous bravery when as a scout to a patrol he worked his way towards the enemy's line with the greatest gallantry and determination,' the citation reads, 'in spite of continuous fire from hostile snipers at close range. These snipers he stalked and killed. Later his patrol was similarly held up, and again he disposed of the snipers.

'When during the subsequent withdrawal of the patrol it was observed that a party of the enemy were endeavouring to outflank them, Private Barratt at once volunteered to cover the retirement, and this he succeeded in accomplishing. His accurate shooting caused many casualties to the enemy, and prevented their advance.

'Throughout the enterprise he was under heavy machine-gun and rifle fire, and his splendid example of coolness and daring was beyond all praise. After safely regaining our lines, this very gallant soldier was killed by a shell.'

TOP SCORE

By a wide margin, the highest-scoring Allied sniper of World War I was Canadian Corporal Francis Pegahmagabow. A Native American of the Ojibwa tribe from the Parry Island Band in Ontario, 'Peggy', as he was commonly called, survived the war with a remarkable tally of 378 kills. He enlisted in the armed forces in 1914, was wounded at least once, and returned home only after the armistice had been concluded. He was a leader in his local community after the war and died in 1952 at the age of 61.

Another highly successful sniper in the service of Canada was Lance Corporal Henry Norwest, who himself fell victim to a sniper's bullet in August 1918 after reaching a total of 115 confirmed kills. After entering the army in January 1915

under his real name, Henry Louie, he was discharged for misconduct three months later. He then joined the army again, this time under the name Norwest. Following the seizure of Vimy Ridge, Henry was cited for 'great bravery, skill and initiative in sniping the enemy after the capture of the Peak.... By his activity he saved a great number of our men's lives.'

Norwest was, in fact, a character somewhat larger than life. A comrade in the 50th Infantry Battalion wrote, 'Our famous sniper no doubt understood better than most of us the cost of life and the price of death. Henry Norwest carried out his terrible duty superbly because he believed his special skill gave him no choice but to fulfill his indispensable mission. Our 50th sniper went about his work with passionate dedication and showed complete detachment from everything while he

Above: *In October 1918, during the waning days of World War I, a British sniper peers through his telescopic sight. The rubble of a devastated French village provides excellent cover.*

was in the line.... Yet when we had the rare opportunity to see our comrade at close quarters, we found him pleasant and kindly, quite naturally one of us, and always an inspiration.'

Often, the men in the ranks were wary of the activity of their own snipers, fearing retribution which could come at a moment's notice. An artillery barrage sent across No Man's Land to silence an individual might take a number of others with him. As the conflict progressed, the sniper achieved a growing notoriety and even a degree of prestige.

Certainly, if there were benefits, there were also heightened risks. A small twitch or a flash of reflected sunlight could mean a swift demise. Prisoners identified as snipers might expect no quarter, given the captor's desire to avenge a fallen comrade.

Nevertheless, the sniper conjured fear, sometimes loathing, and sheer exasperation. In *The Great Push: An Episode of the Great War*, author Patrick MacGill remembered such an occurrence.

'Once, when a German sniper potting at our trenches in Vermelles picked off a few of our men, an exasperated English subaltern gripped a Webley revolver and clambered over the parapet. "I'm going to stop that damned sniper," said the young officer. "I'm going to earn the V.C. [Victoria Cross]. Who's coming along with me?" "I'm with you," said Gilhooley, scrambling lazily out into the open with a couple of pet bombs in his hand. "By Jasus! we'll get him out of it!" The two men went forward about [18m] twenty yards, when the officer fell with a bullet through his head. Gilhooley turned round and called back, "Any other officer wantin' to earn the V.C.?" There was no reply: Gilhooley sauntered back, waited in the trench till dusk, when he went across to the sniper's abode with a bomb and "got him out."'

PRESTIGIOUS ELITE

Snipers had an elevated status among their peers in the trenches. As Adrian Gilbert noted, 'On both sides of the line the sniper had acquired an élite status, and was a respected if unpopular figure with his comrades. For men who had the requisite skills, the life of a sniper held certain advantages. Spared the drudgery of ordinary soldiering the sniper held a roving commission; operating independently within his battalion he was able to exercise his own initiative – an opportunity unknown to most soldiers.'

SNIPERS AT GALLIPOLI

In the spring of 1915, soldiers from Britain, France, Australia, and New Zealand landed on the shore of the Gallipoli Peninsula. Their purpose was to facilitate an Allied naval offensive in the Dardanelles, the strait which separates Europe from Asia in the Mediterranean basin, and threaten Constantinople, the capital of Turkey. The landings were on a hostile shore. The Ottoman Turks were aligned with Germany, and they contested the incursion bitterly.

Allied commanders had hoped that a successful operation at Gallipoli would force Turkey to sue for peace and open a supply route to the hard-pressed Russians through the Black Sea. Thousands of miles away from the stagnating Western Front and very near the site of the ancient city of Troy, another contest of attrition and bloody trench warfare developed. The Allies suffered 250,000 casualties, including 46,000 killed, before withdrawing their last units in January 1916.

As in Europe, the soldiers of the Commonwealth found their losses to effective enemy snipers rising early in the campaign. The death toll was often in excess of 20 per day. Colonel A.C. Fergusson, an artillery officer, described a novel Turkish sniper tactic.

'After we had been ashore quite a long time and were well dug-in at "Pifferpore" we always had at least one casualty per night which always occurred in the same place, just opposite our mess,' related Fergusson. 'One night at dusk just after our Doctor had been talking about it, I noticed something white beside the road, just where the casualties occurred. I sent a man to see what it was and he came back with a piece of white cloth. That night there were no casualties at that spot, but the next night there was a piece of white paper there. I had this taken away, again no casualties. After that it was the Mess Orderly's job to look out for and clear away

Below: *During a lull in the fighting at Gallipoli, British soldiers pause to rest in their improvised hilltop defensive position. In the foreground, one 'Tommy' holds a Lee-Enfield SMLE rifle fitted with a scope.*

marks from there every evening at dusk and casualties ceased. The *modus operandi* apparently was, the sniper laid his rifle on or a little to one side of the mark. When he saw it obscured he pulled the trigger, if the target was going one way he missed, if the other, he hit. There was so much rifle fire going on all round, he was not likely to be spotted from his firing position within our lines.'

Armed with German-supplied Mauser rifles, the Turks were also quite proficient in the game of concealment, using both natural cover and manmade camouflage. Although some soldiers reported active female snipers at Gallipoli, there remains some conjecture as to the authenticity of these sightings.

BILLY SING AND 'ABDUL THE TERRIBLE'

Prolific author Ion Idriess served with the Australian 5th Light Horse Regiment at Gallipoli and recorded the death of one sniper victim in his diary. 'He was a little infantry lad, quite a boy, with snowy hair that looked comical above his clean singlet. I was going for water. He stepped out of a dugout and walked down the path ahead whistling. I was puffing the old pipe, while carrying a dozen water bottles. Just as we were crossing Shrapnel Gully he suddenly flung up his water bottles, wheeled around, and stared for one startled second, even as he crumpled to my feet. In seconds his hair was scarlet, his clean white singlet all crimson.'

Idriess worked as a spotter for another member of the 5th Light Horse, Trooper Billy Sing. With a confirmed total of 150 kills, and a true tally which may have reached over 200, Sing became a scourge of the Gallipoli trenches during Allied counter-sniper operations. Before the war, Sing had been a member of a rifle club and an accomplished kangaroo hunter. In the *Brisbane Courier Mail*, author Brian Tate wrote of Sing's encounter with a Turkish master sniper.

'As the campaign moved on and Sing's persistence and accuracy took their toll, it was inevitable that a response would come from the Turks. At first, orthodox military methodology was applied to put an end to the Australian who had taken out as many as nine of the enemy in a single day. One such Turkish reaction saw Sing's growing confidence shaken by a very near miss, one quiet morning in late August at Chatham's.

'Billy and his observer, on this occasion, Trooper Tom Sheehan, sat silently surveying the enemy trenches, waiting for an unthinking mouse to appear. Their eyes and telescope swept the ground to the front, seeking the almost imperceptible giveaway signs. A quick hazy puff of vapour from a weapon discharge, the unguarded tell-tale movement of an arm or body.

CASUALTIES OF WAR

The stark horror of war was apparent to all who fought in the Gallipoli campaign, which lasted from the Allied landings in April 1915 until the final evacuations in early 1916. While serving as a lieutenant in the Turkish Army, Mehmed Fasih was shocked to view the corpse of a sniper victim:

'[The] top of his skull and brain are gone,' wrote the Turk. 'Inside of head, completely empty. Part of spinal cord visible. Blue veins dangle. Roots of eyeballs exposed.... The sight boggles the mind.'

'A Turkish marksman with a similar intent seized upon a sudden and inadvertent movement in the Australian sniping team and fired on them. His shot passed through Sheehan's telescope, end to end, wounding the Australian in both hands, before entering his mouth and coming out his left cheek. The almost-spent bullet travelled on, completing its pernicious run by striking Sing in the right shoulder.... It was another week before Billy Sing was physically and psychologically able to ... face the newly respected Turkish snipers once more.

Left: *An Australian light horseman fires over the parapet of his fortification at a Turkish periscope. Sometimes firing over the parapet proved safe, with quick aim and only one shot.*

'The next attempt by the Turks to clear their left flank of the unrelenting Australian sniper was more formidable. Reports of these efforts came to light later, from accounts by Turkish prisoners, as well as translated extracts from diaries removed from the bodies of their dead. The Turks sent for their own champion near the centre of the front line.

'Already decorated by the sultan for his proficiency, the Turkish sniper – whom Australians called "Abdul the Terrible" – probably relished the challenge. Abdul brought with him a determination which matched Billy Sing's.... Each fresh description of yet another sniping victim would see Abdul quickly sent to the spot.... Reconstructing each fatal shot, the Turk determined the bullet's angle of trajectory from the entry and exit wounds.... With each calculation, the Turkish sniper drew with his eye a line which ended at an area of the Australian trenches on Harris Ridge. Eventually a pattern began to emerge. His gaze consistently returned to fix on one specific location, a small rise on the heights at Chatham's Post. At last he had found the lair of the too-efficient Australian killer ...

'Despite tempting targets which appeared from time to time, the Turkish sniper held his fire.... Eventually, however, his persistence paid off. He returned to the

Below: Flanked by a pair of ANZAC soldiers, a captured Turkish sniper is paraded before the camera wearing his improvised camouflage. The effectiveness of advanced fieldcraft such as this can greatly improve sniper survivability.

CAMOUFLAGE

The History of The Norfolk Regiment relates the Allied soldiers' experience on the Gallipoli peninsula. 'Beyond the plain a number of stunted oaks, gradually becoming more dense farther inland, formed excellent cover for the enemy's snipers, a mode of warfare at which the Turk was very adept. Officers and men were continually shot down, not only by rifle fire from advanced posts of the enemy, but by men, and even women, behind our own firing line, especially in the previous attacks. The particular kind of tree in this part, a stunted oak, lends itself to concealment, being short with dense foliage. Here the sniper would lurk, with face painted green, and so well hidden as to defy detection. Others would crouch in the dense brushwood, where anyone passing could be shot with ease. When discovered, these snipers had in their possession enough food and water for a considerable period, as well as an ample supply of ammunition.'

Turkish trenches late one evening, certain that he had found his rival and that the new day would see him finally end Sing's winning streak.

'The next morning, Billy and his spotter took up their position. As Sing settled himself in, the observer began his day's first semi-alert yawning frontal sweep with his telescope. Almost immediately the man's movement abruptly ceased and he whispered to his sniper that he already had a target. Sing took the telescope and, glancing towards a point indicated by his spotter, he stared ahead – in the face and rifle-muzzle of Abdul the Terrible. Carefully taking up his rifle, Sing made a final check that nothing would betray their position; then gently eased the loophole cover back and cautiously pushed the weapon forward. The Turk also saw Sing and began his own firing sequence. As he settled the rifle into his shoulder, Abdul drew in a breath and steadily sighted it on Sing. At that moment, a bullet struck the Turk between the eyes.'

After the evacuation from Gallipoli, Sing was transferred to the Western Front, where his efforts to dislodge German snipers at Polygon Wood resulted in the award of the Belgian *Croix de Guerre*. He returned to Australia after the war and died penniless in 1943 at the age of 57.

At the conflict's beginning in 1914, the sniper had been something of a battlefield curiosity. The crucible of war, however, soon made his deadly potential apparent. The accomplished sniper could inflict a telling number of casualties on the enemy, sap his morale, and gather valuable intelligence about dispositions and movements. Despite being relegated to the shadows in peacetime, the sniper re-emerged during a second global conflict a generation later as an integral tactical component of the world's modern armies.

Wary of German snipers, fighters of the French Forces of the Interior, loyal to General Charles de Gaulle, take cover behind trees along a Parisian boulevard, 24 August 1944. Allied forces, led by the Free French 2nd Armoured Division commanded by Major General Leclerc, liberated Paris the next day. The liberation of the French capital was hastened by an open rebellion by Parisians against the Nazis in the days preceding the German surrender of the city.

CHAPTER THREE

WAR IN THE WEST

World War II was the largest and costliest armed conflict in history.
On countless occasions, fighting on a global scale was reduced to single combat,
a skilled sniper stalking an equally determined enemy. Village by village,
'Fortress Europe' was freed from Nazi tyranny.

Four years of brutal occupation were over. Paris, the City of Light, was at last liberated. On 25 August 1944, tanks of the Free French 2nd Armoured Division rolled into their capital city. German soldiers were rounded up; collaborators were identified and received swift justice. The following day, as final victory seemed so near that summer, the personification of the spirit of France, General Charles de Gaulle, returned to Paris.

Exiled in Britain since the fall of France in 1940, de Gaulle had refused to follow the path of the collaborationist Vichy government. He had led the organized expatriate resistance to the Nazis, and his supreme moment of triumph was at hand. At 3 p.m. on 26 August, a huge victory parade commenced. Thousands lined the route as the tall, resolute figure of de Gaulle, in full uniform, strode down the Champs Elysées.

As the leader approached the Place de la Concorde, a rifle's report rang through the crowded streets. In seconds, spectators ran for cover, weapons were drawn, and shots were being fired indiscriminately. De Gaulle, however, continued on undeterred. When he arrived at the cathedral of Notre Dame, bullets began flying once again. With great self-assurance and singular purpose, the general remained unfazed. He walked nearly 60m (200ft) down the aisle and took his seat. Such a display of coolness under fire impressed all those who saw it. The media recounted the story of de Gaulle's bravado. A BBC reporter confessed, 'He walked straight ahead in what appeared to me to be a hail of fire, without hesitation, his shoulders flung back. It was the most extraordinary example of courage that I've ever seen.' Another reporter said the performance ensured that de Gaulle 'had France in the palm of his hand'.

Indeed, France had its hero, its modern post-war leader. Few men could stand in the sites of a sniper and not flinch.

Between the world wars, military establishments around the globe absorbed the rapid technological advances which had been achieved during the

GEWEHR 41

Country of Origin	Germany
Calibre	7.92mm (0.31in)
Overall length	1124mm (44.25in)
Barrel length	546mm (21.5in)
Weight	4.4kg (9.7lb)

conflict of 1914–18. The tank, the submarine and the aircraft were three weapons which were destined to play an even greater role in the warfare of the future. The sniper, on the other hand, was viewed by many military minds as something of an anachronism, a relic of the static warfare in the trenches. A war-weary and financially strapped Britain and an isolationist America seemed loath to embrace the purveyors of such an art in their armed forces, which were greatly reduced in strength and numbers.

Amid the turmoil of civil unrest and economic calamity, Weimar Germany devalued the relevance of the sniper. Author Martin Pegler wrote, '… Germany all but dismissed the sniper as tactically irrelevant. In a memorandum from the German Chief of Army Command dated 5 December 1931 it was recommended that "Telescopic sight carbines should be used up. Parts for mounting the telescopic sight as well as spare parts … will no longer be kept in stock. Telescopic sight carbines in need of repair will be exchanged for rifles".'

Throughout the 1930s, the Soviet Union was the only major power to maintain a commitment to a relatively large, highly trained sniper force. The British Army had curtailed its sniper training and reduced the number of qualified personnel to only eight in an entire battalion. In the United States, the army maintained no formal sniper training programme, while only a handful of marines were designated for the purpose.

THE VALUE OF THE SNIPER

Initially, the swift Nazi *Blitzkrieg* tactics which overwhelmed western Poland, France and the Low Countries were not conducive to sniper operations. Nevertheless, it was quickly becoming apparent to both Allied and Axis military commanders that the sniper remained a viable weapon of war. The sniper had been more than an annoyance to the enemy. True enough, he had inflicted casualties, but he had also gathered important intelligence, identified high-value targets and served as an early warning system. Although a faster pace of combat might present different challenges, the motivated, well-trained, roving sniper might again prove to be a valuable asset.

By 1940, the British had established a sniper school at Bisley. Others were to follow, and, as they had in the previous war, the Lovat Scouts again provided much of the training of British snipers. The standard British sniper rifle remained the P14 Mk I until it was replaced by the 0.303in (7.7mm) calibre Enfield No. 4 Mk I.

In Germany, the *Waffen SS* undertook a sniper training programme at the request of its leader, *Reichsführer* Heinrich Himmler. A sniper school was established at Zossen, and numerous such programmes were operated by *Luftwaffe* field units and the regular army within the Third Reich. In 1935, the German Army was equipped with the *Karabiner* 98K rifle, which was a shortened version of the World War I vintage Mauser *Gewehr* 98. Later, the semiautomatic 7.92mm (0.31in) *Gewehr* 43 entered service ostensibly as a sniper weapon. However, it never proved as popular as the 98K, which, equipped with telescopic sights, was preferred by most German snipers throughout World War II.

In the United States, virtually no army sniper training took place, with the exception of a short course at Camp Perry in Ohio. The standard sniper rifle remained the 0.30in (7.62mm) calibre Springfield Model 1903 A-1, which was followed by the A-4 variant used in Europe and later the C and D versions of the 0.30in (7.62mm) calibre M-1 Garand, which included a conical flash suppressor,

Below: *Secreted in a cornfield, a German sniper armed with a scoped Mauser rifle peers toward the enemy. He is accompanied by an infantryman armed with a submachine gun and a Panzerfaust anti-tank weapon.*

heavier barrel, telescopic sight and a cheek pad. According to Pegler, the US Marines trained their best marksmen informally for a scout-sniper role until a programme was established at Fort Bragg, North Carolina, in late 1942.

The deadly business of sniping gained momentum with the pace of the war in the West. The British did employ some snipers successfully during the short-lived defence of Norway and prior to the evacuation of the expeditionary force at Dunkirk in May 1940. One of these was Private Edgar Rabbets of the 5th Northants, who preferred to ply his craft alone rather than in the company of a spotter (see box).

COMMANDO SNIPERS

In the British Army, the best marksmen among the elite commando units were trained to recognize that shape, shadow, shine and silhouette were four elements which could betray the sniper's position. Up to 5000 commandos eventually completed a programme which grew steadily in intensity and urgency.

In the early hours of the morning of 18 August 1942, the Allies launched Operation Jubilee, a large raid on the coastal town of Dieppe in occupied France. The operation, which ended disastrously, was carried out primarily by Canadian troops, British No. 3 and No. 4 Commandos and a handful of US Army Rangers. The success of the raid depended on the element of surprise, which was lost early on with the discovery of the Allied flotilla by a German convoy.

The commandos' objective was to silence batteries at either end of the landing beaches, No. 3 to the east at Berneval and No. 4 to the west at Varengeville. The landing craft of No. 3 Commando came under attack by German E-boats and armed trawlers which had been escorting a tanker. Several of the British vessels were sunk, and about 50 per cent of the No. 3 Commando contingent was put out of action. Five thousand Canadian soldiers landed in the face of heavy fire at Dieppe, as an alerted German garrison swept the beaches from reinforced positions on the cliffs above. Much of the planned preliminary bombardment had been cancelled. Intelligence reports that the area was lightly defended proved to be erroneous, and nearly 4000 Allied soldiers were killed, wounded or captured. The lone bright spot for the Allies at Dieppe was the performance of No. 4 Commando. Attacking in two groups, one commanded by Lord Lovat and the other by Captain Derek Mills-Roberts, the commandos silenced the Varengeville battery of six 150mm (5.9in) guns and managed to escape. An observer who accompanied them wrote of his experience two days later.

BETWEEN EYE AND EAR

'As a general rule, Rabbets preferred to use his talents in fieldcraft to get in close to his targets, thereby improving his chances of a first-round kill. Rabbets was an accomplished marksman, and was capable of gaining a head shot up to a range of [91m] 100 yards from a standard [7.7mm] .303 Lee-Enfield. Rabbets generally went for the head rather than the torso: "it was the best place to kill them; it's a nice white target and you know once you've hit him in the head he's dead. It's as good a target as any, you hit him just below the helmet in between his eye and his ear"'.

Adrian Gilbert, *Sniper*

'"Like to come up and see what's going on above?" said the signals officer. We climbed the steps. "I can't guarantee there won't be any German snipers about", he added cheerfully, as we walked along the bottom of the gully … He was right, as I found out a little later as I passed several times up and down the gully carrying messages or mortar shells. Snipers seemed to be the Germans' favourite defence immediately along the coast. They were responsible for most of our remarkably few casualties…. Just as I got back to the gully stairs a bullet or two began to whistle past. "That saucy sniper", said a Navy signaller, "is too bloody cocky".'

The observer continued, 'Beyond the woods … there was a stretch of open field, and beyond that lay the barbed wire round the howitzers. It was carelessly laid wire which gave our men little trouble, but the battery defenders knew how to fight. To get at them the attackers had to cross open ground under fire from carefully concealed snipers. There fell two Commando officers, one killed and one seriously

Below: Canadian survivors of the ill-fated 18 August 1942 raid on the French coastal town of Dieppe mill about after returning to safety in England. In the foreground is Lord Lovat, the British officer who led No. 4 Commando in the attack on the Varengeville battery.

Above: *In the*
aftermath of the Dieppe
raid, German soldiers
survey the scene of
battle. Canadian dead
litter the beach alongside
the hulk of a disabled
Churchill tank. Of the
5000 Allied soldiers
who took part in the
raid, almost 4000 were
either killed or captured.

wounded, and several men.... Sniping from his office window was "*Hauptmann* and *Batterie Führer*" Schoeler, the battery C.O. A trooper kicked in the door, sprayed him with tommy-gun bullets. "Couldn't take him prisoner", he said. "It was him or me".'

Three sniper teams were included in the commando units, and those of No. 4 set to work from distances up to about 228m (250 yards) from the Varengeville battery. Mills-Roberts and two snipers reached a barn and climbed into its loft. From there, they could see each of the guns and the crews which serviced them. In *Dieppe 1942*, Ronald Atkin relates their accomplishment.

'The first sniper's bullet was to be a signal for all-out fire to be opened on the Germans and Mills-Roberts gave the order to proceed: "The marksman settled himself on a table, taking careful aim. These Bisley chaps are not to be hurried. At last the rifle cracked. It was a bullseye and one of the Master Race took a toss into the gun pit. His comrades looked shocked and surprised … It seemed rather like shooting one of the members of a church congregation from the organ loft".

'The Germans reacted quickly. A flak tower on stilts sprayed the wood with tracer and mortars caused casualties among the Commandos around the perimeter wire. The flak tower was silenced by an anti-tank rifle and soon the raiders brought into action their own [50.8mm] 2-in. mortar, operated by Troop Sgt-Major Jimmy Dunning with spectacular results. The third shot struck a stack of cordite which ignited with a mighty explosion.

'Gleefully, the Commandos sniped at the battery crews frantically trying to extinguish the fires started by the explosion. The most daring was L/Cpl Dick Mann who, his hands and face painted green, crawled forward over open ground with a telescopic rifle and sniped at the crews from a fully exposed position.'

NORTH AFRICA AND ITALY

The first major US offensive action against the Nazis was Operation Torch, the landings in North Africa, on 8 November 1942. Following his victory at El Alamein on the Egyptian frontier, British General Bernard Montgomery and the Eighth Army pursued the *Afrika Korps* of Field Marshal Erwin Rommel westward over thousands of miles of desert. American troops under General George S. Patton Jr would follow the 'Torch' landings with an eastward advance, trapping the Germans between the two Allied forces. By May 1943, it was over. The remnants of the German Army in North Africa had surrendered.

During World War II in the West, the sniper was engaged in the deserts of North Africa, the mountains of Italy, the hedgerow country of France and the arctic climate of Norway. Urban warfare was common in countless towns and villages. At times, even areas which were considered relatively safe became dangerous, as the US Army history of the Nurse Corps in World War II relates.

'The Army nurses who participated in the North African invasion at first had little conception of the realities of battle and were unfamiliar with military procedures. One nurse at the Arzew hospital became so incensed at snipers firing into the windows of the hospital and endangering the patients that she had to be forcibly restrained from going outside to "give them a piece of her mind".'

A British veteran of North Africa remembered a mopping-up operation against isolated pockets of Germans holding out near the Mediterranean coast. 'The wood ran for quite a way up the hillside ... it was here that some fanatic Germans were holding up the advance of our troops along the sea road, causing casualties from the sniping from the trees. A tank with its gun pointed into the woods was in position at the foot of the bank. The turret of the tank opened and the officer informed us to be careful as the woods were full of snipers.

'We deployed through the trees and started to ascend the thickly covered ground. Then a shot rang out and one of the Guardsmen in front dropped to the ground. We flung ourselves to the grassy hillside and then took view of our surroundings.

'In the trees just above us, we could see slight movement. Our officer crawled along to us and told us to spread out and upon his signal to spray the upper branches of the trees with bren gun fire and rifle fire. At the signal we commenced firing into

DANGEROUS WORK

Combat lineman Norton Hubbard was a member of the US Army Signal Corps in North Africa. In the book *The Hero Next Door Returns*, Norton recalled an encounter with a German sniper while on the job.
'A signalman's task was complicated by land mines, snipers and poor rations. I was shot at by a sniper near Mateur. I was on a telegraph pole and he hit the insulator about a foot from my head on the other side of the pole. I dropped to the ground and went through a railroad tunnel and didn't go back.'

the trees. The noise was deafening ... with about forty Guardsmen firing away it seemed nothing could still be alive in the trees. We were darting about firing up in the air and getting results. Already bodies had started to fall from the leafy branches above. I saw a grey clad figure drop out of the tree in front of me and land right on top of a Guardsman who jumped up as if shot and fired into the body of the German. In about half an hour we had cleared the wood of all enemy resistance.'

HARD SLOG

By September 1943, the Allies had landed at Salerno and begun the painful push up the Italian boot. The fighting in Italy would last until the final days of the war in Europe, and the advance frequently bogged down before strong, prepared German lines of defence. Often, snipers on both sides found themselves in combat situations similar to that in the trenches of World War I.

Below: *Battling their way through Sicily in the summer of 1943, British soldiers survey a seemingly deserted street in the city of Messina. A sniper might lurk in any doorway or window.*

LEE-ENFIELD NO. 4 MK I

Country of Origin	Great Britain
Calibre	0.303in (7.7mm)
Overall length	1129mm (44.4in)
Barrel length	640mm (25.2in)
Weight	4.14kg (9.12lb)

Slipping into the contested area between opposing lines or infiltrating into enemy territory, the sniper and his companion observer hunted their quarry with telling accuracy. In *One Shot-One Kill*, authors Charles Sasser and Craig Roberts wrote of one such foray by US Army Sergeant John Fulcher.

'We snipers adopted a tactic the Nazis sometimes used. Slipping from our lines before daylight, we located a hill or ridge within range of a road or trail inside enemy-occupied territory, divided it into sectors for each two-man team – sniper and spotter – and then settled down to wait for whatever came along …

'I spotted troops coming at the end of the road where it hazed into the horizon. I nudged my partner and nodded in their direction…. Through binoculars, I could tell they were green replacements. Their uniforms were still a crisp gray green; their jackboots kicking up little spurts of dust still shone. They left a cloud of dust hanging in their wake….

'As cool as could be, I cross-haired the officer and shot him through the belly. He looked momentarily surprised. He plopped down on his butt in the middle of the road. The report of the shot reached him as he fell over onto his back. He was dead by the time I brought my rifle down out of recoil and picked him up again in my scope. His legs were drumming on the road, but he was dead. His body just didn't know it yet.

'The other krauts were so green they didn't know enough to scatter for cover until my partner got in his licks by knocking down one more. Even then, they behaved more like quail than combat troops. They hid in the drainage ditches and in some shell craters, their heads bobbing up…. I figured I could have drilled two or three more, but I held my fire. It wouldn't do to be pinpointed, even by green troops …'

'The company reorganized without making an attempt to find us…. As soon as the Germans swept around a distant bend in the road, they were greeted by the twin *Crack! Crack!* of two more rifle shots as they entered another Yank team's sector.'

Slugging their way toward Rome, the capital of Fascist Italy, Allied forces stalled before the formidable, well-prepared German defences of the Gustav Line. In January 1944, at the insistence of British Prime Minister Winston Churchill, an amphibious operation codenamed 'Shingle' was launched to outflank the German positions. American landings at the resort town of Anzio behind the Germans were intended to link up with a British thrust to breach the Gustav Line and clear the way to Rome. Rather than a lightning thrust, Operation Shingle deteriorated into a protracted battle of attrition as German reinforcements contained the Anzio beachhead. Counterattacks threatened to push the Americans back into the sea before the Allies prevailed. One such counterattack occurred against troops of the US 45th Infantry Division at a location dubbed the 'Overpass'. In his book *The Rock of Anzio*, author Flint Whitlock recounts the heroism of one 45th Division sniper.

'Another soldier who earned [Sergeant Robert J.] Franklin's praise was Kenneth Kindig, a sniper with I company, whom Franklin called "a one-man army".

'Kindig recalled that he and his buddies tried digging foxholes near the Overpass but "… you'd dig down about a foot and hit water, so we never *had* much protection. The company command post was on a little higher ground so they could dig down about [1m] three feet. We were in front of the Overpass and about [4.5 to 9.1m] five to ten yards apart. We were scattered pretty good so that if an artillery shell came in, it wouldn't get all of us. I was in a foxhole near the company command post when the Germans let loose with an artillery barrage. One of their shells landed right next to my foxhole and caved it in on me. The shell didn't go off; it was a dud. If it had gone off, it would have blown me right out of there".

'Kindig had been issued a brand-new rifle with a telescopic sight and was performing sniper duties. "We had barbed wire out there and the Germans were trying to get over it and under it and around it. I was on the outskirts with that sniper rifle and they were coming up through some drainage ditches at us. I picked them off before they could get around to us." Kindig was credited with killing or wounding twenty-five of the enemy. He was soon put out of action himself during a brief lull in the fighting.'

Kindig was wounded by shrapnel from a mortar round and later received the Bronze Star for his actions at the Overpass. The mortar round which sent him to the field hospital also destroyed the sniper rifle.

D-DAY SNIPERS

On 6 June 1944, Operation Overlord, the largest combined air, land and sea operation in history up to that time, commenced. British, American and Canadian troops landed on five beaches, 'Gold', 'Juno', 'Sword', 'Utah' and 'Omaha', along the coast of Normandy. The successful D-Day assault against Adolf Hitler's vaunted Atlantic Wall defences heralded the beginning of the end for Nazi Germany. Eleven months of bitter fighting, however, still lay ahead. Stubborn resistance from snipers

'I was on the outskirts with that sniper rifle and they were coming up through some drainage ditches at us. I picked them off before they could get around us.'

Sniper Kenneth Kindig

was encountered from the beginning, and often extreme measures – even artillery – were employed to clear the advance. Major R.R. Reynolds of the King's Shropshire Light Infantry wrote of his D-Day experiences in the vicinity of 'Sword' Beach for the unit's regimental journal.

'Ahead, X Coy. were meeting serious trouble from snipers in the north end of the village of Beuville. This consisted of strong stone buildings, interspersed with walled orchards – a paradise for determined marksmen fighting a delaying action. And delay us they did, so Major Slatter, impatient because X Coy. seemed held up, walked up the road to the centre of the bother. Here he fought a private battle with some snipers, and was seriously wounded in the arm. Nevertheless, he managed to give us a picture of the situation before he collapsed and was evacuated, protesting. Capt. Rylands took over, and went forward to Major Thornycroft for a palaver, which was joined by the C.O. Direct progress down the middle of the village looked like being a slow and costly affair; the civilians refused to evacuate themselves, and at that early

Below: Their helmets festooned with camouflage, British infantrymen armed with Sten guns and Lee-Enfield No. 4 Mk I rifles clear outbuildings on a farm in Normandy.

'I wouldn't
venture out
there, fellas.
This sniper's
got talent.'

*Barry Pepper
portraying Private
Jackson in* Saving
Private Ryan

stage we were too soft-hearted to shell their homes – a proceeding which might have facilitated our advance considerably.'

HARD LANDING

The first priority for the Allied ground troops was advancing inland from the exposed positions on the landing beaches where the German defenders had pre-sighted artillery, mortar and machine-gun positions to create interlocking fields of fire. The most serious resistance was encountered by troops of the US 1st Infantry Division and an attached regimental combat team of the 29th Infantry Division at 'Omaha' Beach. In *June 6, 1944 – The Voices of D-Day*, Gerald Astor related the memories of Sergeant Bob Slaughter, a machine gunner with the 29th.

'"Snipers, machine guns, and 88s interrupted movement on the road to Vierville", remembered Slaughter. "The column took cover and waited for an officer or noncom with the initiative to collar a few riflemen and clear the obstacle.... Following an exchange of fire, three or four enemy soldiers appeared waving white flags, hands over heads, yelling, '*Kamerad!*' With them appeared a young French female civilian whom we suspected of collaboration. Thinking she was one of the deadly snipers, we didn't treat her or the other prisoners gently. I doubt they made it back to the beach alive".

'A few weeks after his torment at "Omaha" Beach, Slaughter escaped serious injury as a sniper's bullet pierced the bill of his steel helmet and inflicted a bloody graze.'

In sharp contrast to the carnage at 'Omaha', the American landings at 'Utah' Beach faced much weaker opposition, partially because the 4th Infantry Division landed in the wrong place. Brigadier General Theodore Roosevelt, Jr, assistant division commander of the 4th and son of the famous American president, decided against sending remaining units onto the original beach and diverted them to his position in the quieter sector. His decision to 'start the war from here', and his subsequent actions in Normandy earned him the Congressional Medal of Honor.

John Ausland was a member of the 4th Division on D-Day. Years later he wrote *The Ivy Leaves*, a book whose title references the division's insignia, and included a letter home describing his 'Utah' Beach drama.

'... At last we got our unit off the bomb torn beach,' Ausland wrote to his family, 'and away from the constant shelling. For the rest of the day there are only momentary recollections. Tough paratroopers wandering about, killing German snipers.... The sniper (we later learned he was [68.5m] 75 yards from our command post) who shot at us all day without hitting anyone. He was killed by a paratrooper who happened across him.... These and a hundred other events made up D-Day for me.'

Certainly, many of the snipers which Allied soldiers encountered during the fighting in Western Europe were not dedicated solely to the sniper craft. In his classic work *With British Snipers to the Reich*, Captain Clifford Shore points out that

SNIPERS IN MOVIES

American filmmakers have included dramatic World War II sniper encounters in several films. Two of the most memorable occur in the 1968 film *Anzio* and Steven Spielberg's gripping *Saving Private Ryan* (see picture below) three decades later.

In *Anzio*, war correspondent Robert Mitchum becomes a combat soldier during an encounter with German snipers, one of whom searches for Mitchum and asks aloud, '*Wo bist du, Amerikaner?*' Mitchum, meanwhile, has worked his way behind the enemy sniper and replies, 'Right here, German!' before firing a killing burst.

In *Saving Private Ryan*, Barry Pepper, portraying sniper Jackson, warns his buddies that the German sniper who has just fatally wounded another member of his squad has 'talent'. Jackson and the German sniper play cat and mouse for a few moments before the American puts a bullet through his enemy's scope.

a large number of these were trained riflemen who were nevertheless resourceful and willing to confront the enemy singly or with a small number of comrades. Ad hoc sniping was commonplace on both sides. John Bistrica was a rifleman with the 1st Infantry Division in Normandy. He related such a story to Gerald Astor in *June 6, 1944 – The Voices of D-Day*.

'Mostly we fought snipers …' Bistrica recalled. 'A lieutenant, who was a ninety-day wonder, called me to his CP [command post], gave me a sniper's rifle, told me to find a tree and start picking off Germans…. As I started to leave, Captain Briggs, our CO, saw me. "Bistrica, where are you going with that weapon?" I told him. Briggs said, "Give me that rifle and go back to the lieutenant to get your M–1 and tell him I want to see him".'

For centuries, Norman farms and fields had been separated by long, imposing mounded hedgerows. These natural barriers were several feet high and usually overgrown with trees and other vegetation. In the weeks which followed D-Day, the fighting through this hedgerow country – a type of terrain known as *bocage* – was

particularly bloody. Each successive country lane was bordered by a potential strongpoint manned by German riflemen and machine gunners. The *bocage* was also a haven for the well-trained sniper.

SNIPER FEAR

Writing for the Normandy Project, undertaken by students at Coral Gables Senior High School, Florida, Mayra Cruz noted a common occurrence. 'German snipers were a particular source of fear. The experience of a platoon leader in the 9th Division illustrates how green troops can react under fire: "One of the fatal mistakes made by the infantry replacements is to hit the ground and freeze when fired upon.

Once I ordered a squad to advance from one hedgerow to another. During the movement one man was shot by a sniper firing one round. The entire squad hit the ground and froze. They were picked off, one by one, by the same sniper".'

Nearly two months after D-Day, the frustrated Allies finally succeeded in effecting a breakout from the hedgerow country and made a spectacular dash across France to the German frontier. Operation Cobra, the breakout itself, involved the concentrated bombing of German positions in the vicinity of the town of Saint-Lô. The bombing was followed by a rapid thrust through German lines. In spite of the preparations, combat was heavy. Harper Coleman of the 4th Division told Astor about his recollections of the days prior to the breakout.

'During this period, we lost quite a few people,' Coleman commented. 'How anyone made it I still do not know. I saw one battalion commander killed by a sniper as he stood near our position. A member of our squad was killed by a sniper, and a bullet came across my shoulder, cutting the top of my hand.'

In Normandy, proficient German snipers took such a toll on Allied officers that many began to disguise their badges of rank. Authors quoted in Gilbert's *Sniper* conveyed the perception of the menace.

'At night snipers crept through the positions, to open fire ... on parties coming up from the rear. Dozens of bloody little battles were fought behind the forward positions. The snipers were everywhere. Officers, their chosen prey, learned to conceal all

Opposite: His helmet perched on the barrel of his rifle, a GI tries to draw fire from a German sniper in Normandy. At times a single well-hidden marksman could hold up a large formation for hours.

'Here in
Normandy the
Germans have
gone in for
sniping in a
wholesale
manner. There
are snipers
everywhere.'

*Correspondent
Ernie Pyle*

distinguishing marks, to carry rifles like their own men instead of their accustomed pistols, not to carry maps or field glasses, to wear pips on their sleeves instead of conspicuously on their shoulders.'

Captain Shore recalled the death of one commander in Normandy just a few days after arriving. 'I saw an officer leave the assembly area in a Jeep, smiling broadly, driven by an harassed faced driver. A few minutes later the Jeep returned with the officer dead, a neat hole being drilled in the centre of his forehead. "Sniper" muttered the driver hoarsely. I must admit that it gave me, and the others, a shock.'

The irony of the sniper's lot in World War II lay in the acknowledgement that he was, at the same time, revered and reviled. Snipers were considered to give no quarter and therefore received none. Upper echelon commanders were known to turn a blind eye to the out-of-hand execution of snipers who were captured. Correspondent Ernie Pyle, whose fame grew steadily as the war progressed, captured the essence of the American fighting man's feeling. Reporting for the Scripps Howard newspaper chain, Pyle wrote: 'SOMEWHERE IN FRANCE, June 26, 1944 – Sniping, as far as I know, is recognized as a legitimate means of warfare. And yet there is something sneaky about it that outrages the American sense of fairness.

'I had never sensed this before we landed in France and began pushing the Germans back. We have had snipers before – in Bizerte and Cassino and lots of other places. But always on a small scale.

'Here in Normandy the Germans have gone in for sniping in a wholesale manner. There are snipers everywhere. There are snipers in trees, in buildings, in piles of wreckage, in the grass. But mainly they are in the high, bushy hedgerows that form the fences of all the Norman fields and line every roadside and lane. It is perfect sniping country.

US ARMY *COMBAT LESSONS*

In an effort to educate its soldiers about the perils of hedgerow fighting, the U.S. Army published *Combat Lessons*, periodic articles concerning the nature of combat. One such article offered sound advice: 'The German soldiers had been given orders to stay in their positions.... Some of their snipers stayed hidden for 2 to 5 days after a position had been taken and then "popped up" suddenly ... to take the shot for which they had been waiting. We found fire crackers with slow burning fuses left by snipers and AT gun crews in their old positions when they moved. These exploded at irregular intervals, giving the impression that the position was still occupied by enemy forces. High losses among tank commanders have been caused by German snipers. Keep buttoned up, as the German rifleman concentrates on such profitable targets. After an action the turret of the commander's tank is usually well marked with rifle bullets.'

M-1 GARAND

Country of Origin	United States
Calibre	0.30in (7.62mm)
Overall length	1107mm (43.6in)
Barrel length	609mm (24in)
Weight	4.31kg (9.5lb)

'Every mile we advance there are dozens of snipers left behind us. They pick off our soldiers one by one as they walk down the roads or across the fields. It isn't safe to move into a new bivouac area until the snipers have been cleaned out. The first bivouac I moved into had shots ringing through it for a full day before all the hidden gunmen were rounded up. It gives you the same spooky feeling that you get on moving into a place you suspect of being sown with mines.

'In the past our soldiers would talk about the occasional snipers with contempt and disgust. But here sniping has become important, and taking precautions against it is something we have had to learn and learn fast. One officer friend of mine said: "Individual soldiers have become sniper-wise before, but now we're sniper-conscious as whole units".

'Snipers kill as many Americans as they can, and then when their food and ammunition run out they surrender. To an American, that isn't quite ethical. The average American soldier has little feeling against the average German soldier who has fought an open fight and lost. But his feelings about the sneaking snipers can't very well be put into print. He is learning how to kill the snipers before the time comes for them to surrender ...'

Associated Press reporter Roger Greene watched a pitched gunbattle between German snipers and Allied soldiers engaged in counter-sniper operations while composing a column for newspapers in the United States.

'As I write in the living room of a French chateau, a stealthy manhunt is going on in the rose gardens and bushes immediately outside. A few minutes ago one of our soldiers came to the chateau door and then started back on the front path. A sniper's bullets kicked up dust around his feet and he fell prone in a shallow ditch.

'From a front window a British correspondent and I watched the soldier crawl down the path a scant dozen yards away with the sniper's shots trailing him until he reached the brick wall at the end of the path.

Above: *Camouflaged for winter, an American infantryman takes aim with an M-1 Garand during the Battle of the Bulge in January 1945. Note the camouflaged wrapping around the barrel of the soldier's rifle and sling.*

'Now scores of troops are combing the thick brush around the chateau and bullets are cracking like popcorn all around.

'Last evening ... I crouched on a road between a brick wall and a jeep for nearly two hours, while German snipers who had lain doggo all day sent tracer bullets crackling around us.... One of the German snipers apparently lay hidden within whispering distance during the night, for he began his shooting from a nearby clump of bushes this morning ...

'The manhunt is over. A stocky, bronzed sergeant strides into the room and points significantly to the woods opposite the chateau whence the sniper's bullets have been coming.

'"Got him, the blighter", he says, and then with a grin, "well, what's cooking with you, Yank?"'

NEW KILLING GROUNDS

Following the Normandy breakout, a rapidly deteriorating front-line situation gave German snipers fewer opportunities to inflict casualties. However, the horrific

WAR IN THE WEST

fighting in the Reichswald and the Hürtgen Forest provided new killing grounds for snipers on both sides. During the abortive Operation Market Garden, a combined British–American airborne strike through Holland and toward the Ruhr, the industrial heart of Germany, snipers took their toll. One American officer, Lieutenant Colonel Robert G. Cole, had earned the Congressional Medal of Honor for leading a charge across a bullet-swept causeway during the capture of Carentan in Normandy. Cole, commander of the 3rd Battalion, 502nd Parachute Infantry Regiment, did not live to receive his medal. He was killed by a sniper's bullet weeks later during 'Market Garden'.

By the end of the war in Western Europe, it had become apparent that the sniper had played a significant role in tactical operations, both offensive and defensive. A single, well-placed sniper could render a comparatively large formation of troops immobile for some period of time, as the Germans discovered to their advantage in the mountainous terrain of Italy and the hedgerows of France. He might also cripple its combat effectiveness by killing and wounding officers and junior leaders. The prospect of death by sniper was more real than ever for the common infantryman.

DRINKING TO DEATH

In his book, *With British Snipers to the Reich*, Captain Clifford Shore recalled a particularly productive venture for British snipers in Holland.

'The Battalion were holding one bank of the Nederweet Canal in Holland with the Germans on the opposite bank. The distance between the combatants was only about [22.8m] twenty-five yards and it was possible for the snipers to hear the Germans speaking quite distinctly. There was a very high bank on each side of the canal and although the Battalion snipers waited patiently for hours on end Jerry was very careful, and remained in the safety of his own towering bank. But one afternoon the snipers' patience was amply rewarded, since for some reason or other the Germans decided to have a celebration, and proceeded to get really drunk. The first Hun to be accounted for had a bottle of wine to his lips and was in the act of taking a long draught. Perhaps that is as good a way to die as any! The shot caused a little consternation in Jerry's camp, but not much. The interpreter from the Battalion Intelligence section was alongside the sniper who had "bumped-off" the imbibing one, and he was delighted to translate the resultant conversation for the edification of the snipers. Immediately after the shot had been fired and the German with the bottle killed, a wine-thickened voice bellowed, "Who in the name of Venus fired that shot?". A reply in a similar voice was, "I don't know, but who's the silly — who's been shot anyway?"

'That afternoon drinking party was very costly for the Hun for before nightfall the snipers had killed five. It was really too easy. One wonders what the German platoon commander thought about it all next morning when he awakened with probably a damned bad head and found that his platoon had indeed been sadly depleted in strength.'

His Tokarev SVT40 automatic rifle at the ready, a Soviet sniper prepares to sight his 3.5X PV scope. Although he wears fur mittens, the trigger finger is uninsulated. This photograph was taken during January 1943, in the latter stages of the battle for Stalingrad. On 30 January Field Marshal von Paulus, commander of the German Sixth Army, surrendered his forces, leading many hundreds of thousands of Axis personnel into captivity.

CHAPTER FOUR

THE EASTERN FRONT

The bitter fighting on the Eastern Front during World War II spawned perhaps the greatest sniper legend of all time. On the Russian steppes and in the rubble-strewn streets of Stalingrad, legions of Red Army and Wehrmacht snipers hunted one another relentlessly.

A telltale twinkle ... a sliver of light ... the crack of a rifle. For the sniper, hours, even days, of monotonous seclusion are punctuated by moments of high drama.

The essence of sniping makes it so. Those who demonstrate the fortitude and hone the skills may be called 'sniper' during peacetime. The finest of these are the ones who survive in wartime. So it was with history's most told and retold story of sniper and counter-sniper. It took place in the rubble of Stalin's city on the Volga as encircling Red Army troops tightened the noose around the beleaguered German Sixth Army.

Numerous heroes and countless legends were born during the five-month battle for Stalingrad from September 1942 to February 1943. One of these involves the struggle to the death between Soviet sniper Vassili Zaitsev and the German officer dispatched to the front to end his remarkable career. To this day, theory and conjecture abound as to the veracity of the story. Some believe that the Soviet propaganda machine, in an exhaustive effort to advance the 'cult of the sniper', fabricated the entire incident. Others say that the events took place as recalled by contemporaries.

Apparently, there is no mention of the incident in any official report, Soviet or German, and the *SS* super-sniper sent to settle the account with Zaitsev has been known as Colonel Heinz Thorwald, Major Konings, and Colonel Erwin Konig. References to this individual's actual existence are obscure at best. He was said to have served as the chief of the *SS* sniper school at Zossen near Berlin.

Senior Sergeant Zaitsev, familiarly called Vasha, had grown up a hunter and shepherd near the village of Elininski in the foothills of the Ural Mountains. As a youth, he had been told by his grandfather to remember a valuable maxim: 'The man of the forest is without fear'. Originally, Zaitsev had served as a petty officer with the Soviet Pacific Fleet. Stationed at Vladivostok, he had been a bookkeeper. This mundane existence, however, was intolerable to him while, thousands of miles to the west, his countrymen were fighting Nazi aggression which threatened to destroy his native land. One of several former naval personnel who volunteered for reassignment to the army, he demonstrated his prowess with the Moisin Nagant Model 1891/30 soon after his arrival at Stalingrad on 20 September 1942, as a member of the 284th Rifle Division. In a single 10-day period, his score against the Germans approached 40.

HERO STATUS

Zaitsev rapidly became a national hero in the Soviet Union. The Soviet propaganda machine touted his exploits, and word spread through the ranks of both armies that

Right: *A Soviet scout uses a periscope to observe enemy movements along a segment of the front lines near Leningrad, September 1942. The periscope allows him to avoid the unwanted attentions of German snipers.*

MOISIN NAGANT MODEL 1891/30

Country of Origin	Soviet Union
Calibre	7.62mm (0.30in)
Overall length	1232mm (48.5in)
Barrel length	729mm (28.7in)
Weight	4kg (8.8lb)

the hunter from the Urals was a deadly practitioner. Enter the shadowy figure of the German sniping master. His mission was simply to rid the *Wehrmacht* of this one-man scourge. Years after the encounter between the two, Zaitsev remembered the nerve-wracking series of events.

'The arrival of the Nazi sniper set us a new task: We had to find him, study his habits and methods, and patiently await the moment for one, and only one, well-aimed shot.

'I knew the style of the Nazi snipers by their fire and camouflage. But the character of the head of the school was still a mystery for me. Our day-by-day observations told us nothing definite. It was difficult to decide in which sector he was operating. He presumably altered his position frequently and was looking for me as carefully as I for him.

'Then something happened. My good friend Morozov was killed, and Sheikin wounded, by a rifle with telescopic sights. Morozov and Sheikin were considered experienced snipers; they had often emerged victorious from the most difficult skirmishes with the enemy. Now, there was no doubt. They had come up against the Nazi "super-sniper" I was looking for.

'At dawn I went out with Nikolai Kulikov to the same positions as our comrades had occupied the previous day. Inspecting the enemy's forward positions, I found nothing new. The day was drawing to a close. Then above a German entrenchment unexpectedly appeared a helmet, moving slowly along a trench. Should I shoot? No! It was a trick: The helmet somehow or other moved unevenly and was presumably being held up by someone helping the sniper, while he waited for me to fire.

'A second day passed. Whose nerves would be stronger? Who would outwit whom?

'On the third day, the political instructor, Danilov, also came with us to the ambush. The day dawned as usual: The light increased and minute by minute the

Above: *Clad in warm winter camouflage, Vassili Zaitsev (left) and two sniper comrades observe German positions in Stalingrad, January 1943. The Soviet authorities created the 'cult of the sniper' to increase morale and offer the Soviet people inspirational heroes to emulate.*

enemy's positions could be distinguished more clearly. Battle started close by, shells hissed over us, but, glued to our telescopic sights, we kept our eyes on what was happening ahead of us.

'"There he is! I'll point him out to you!" suddenly said the political instructor, excitedly. He barely, literally for one second, but carelessly, raised himself above the parapet, but that was enough for the German to hit and wound him.

'For a long time I examined the enemy positions, but could not detect his hiding place. To the left was a tank, out of action, and on the right was a pillbox. Where was he? In the tank? No, an experienced sniper would not take up position there. In the pillbox, perhaps? Not there, either – the embrasure was closed. Between the tank and the pillbox … lay a sheet of iron and a small pile of broken bricks. It had been lying there a long time and we had grown accustomed to it being there. I put myself in the enemy's position and thought – where better for a sniper? One had only to make a firing slit under the sheet of metal, and then creep up to it during the night.

'Yes, he was certainly there, under the sheet of metal in no man's land. I thought I would make sure. I put a mitten on the end of a small plank and raised it. The Nazi fell for it. I carefully let the plank down in the same position as I had raised it and examined the bullet hole. It had gone straight through from the front; that meant that the Nazi was under the sheet of metal.

FINNISH SNIPERS OF THE WINTER WAR, 1939–40

Finnish snipers such as Simo Hayha (below) and Suko Kolkka taught the Red Army an expensive lesson among the dense evergreens of the Karelian Forest. Hayha, who is arguably the highest scoring sniper in history, was a former farmer who killed 505 Soviet soldiers in a nine-month period, earning the nickname of the 'White Death'. Kolkka was credited with more than 400 kills during just over three months of combat. He was marked for elimination but managed to elude more than one Soviet counter-sniper sent to end his career. Kolkka was reported to have shot one of them from a distance of 528m (600 yards) following several days of individual stalking. Both men used Soviet-made Moisin Nagant rifles.

'I took careful aim. The German's head fell back, and the telescopic sights of his rifle lay motionless, glistening in the sun until night fell.'

Soviet sniper Vassili Zaitsev

Above: In a still frame from the movie Enemy At The Gates, *Jude Law, portraying Vassili Zaitsev – the Soviet super-sniper – stands in a railyard, drawing a bead on his target.*

'"There's our viper!" came the quiet voice of Nikolai Kulikov from his hide-out next to mine.

'Now came the question of luring even a part of his head into my sights. It was useless trying to do this straightaway. Time was needed. But I had been able to study the German's temperament. He was not going to leave the successful position he had found. We were therefore going to have to change our position.

'We worked by night. We were in position by dawn. The Germans were firing on the Volga ferries. It grew light quickly and with daybreak the battle developed with new intensity. But neither the rumble of guns nor the bursting of shells and bombs nor anything else could distract us from the job in hand.

'The sun rose. We had decided to spend the morning waiting, as we might have been given away by the sun on our telescopic sights. After lunch our rifles were in the shade and the sun was shining directly on the German's position. At the edge of the sheet of metal something was glittering: an odd bit of glass – or telescopic sights?

'Kulikov carefully, as only the most experienced can do, began to raise his helmet. The German fired. For a fraction of a second Kulikov rose and screamed. The German believed that he had finally got the Soviet sniper he had been hunting for four days, and half raised his head from beneath the sheet of metal. That was what I had been banking on.

'I took careful aim. The German's head fell back, and the telescopic sights of his rifle lay motionless, glistening in the sun until night fell.'

SOVIET SNIPER TRAINING

Among the world's major armed forces, it was the Red Army which maintained the highest degree of sniper training and preparedness between the world wars. This was partially due to the experience of some Soviet military personnel who had advised Republican forces during the Spanish Civil War. It was also the result of a largely pyrrhic victory against Finland during the Winter War of 1939–40, in which the Red Army lost an estimated one million men. The Finns decimated the ranks of invading Soviet divisions, utilizing rapid movement on skis, camouflage and hit-and-run tactics.

The lessons of the Winter War were apparently learned well, as author Martin Pegler illustrates in his book *The Military Sniper Since 1914*. 'Some indication of the losses inflicted by the Russians can be glimpsed from one assault by the German 465th Infantry Regiment in September 1941 on a thickly wooded area. In a few hours they lost 75 dead and 25 missing to what were described as "tree snipers" who melted away as the Germans advanced. The Russians proved to be bitterly stubborn adversaries, well equipped and fanatical in their desire to wreak revenge on the invaders. One German account tells of a single sniper who steadily inflicted casualties on a resting Panzer unit over a five-day period. All attempts to locate him failed. One morning a sharp-eyed German observer saw in the bright cold sunlight what appeared to be smoke coming from a knocked out Russian T-34 tank. Investigation showed it to be the breath of a sniper, who had been living in the tank amongst its dead crew for nearly a week. He had survived by eating the crew's frozen rations and by thawing out their waterbottles under his clothing. There is no record of his fate, but it was doubtless swiftly and ruthlessly administered.'

ENEMY AT THE GATES

The duel between Vassili Zaitsev and his German adversary was the basis for the 2001 movie *Enemy At The Gates*, starring Jude Law, Joseph Fiennes and Bob Hoskins. Actor Ed Harris portrayed the elusive German master sniper, dispatched from his post as commandant of a sniper school to eliminate the Soviet marksman.

Zaitsev, the Soviets claimed, killed as many as 400 Germans before a land mine explosion blinded him. His actual number of kills has also been estimated at 242.

SNIPERS OR SHARPSHOOTERS?

The Soviet definition of sniping differed somewhat from those of other armies, to the degree that snipers of the Red Army were expected to conduct general sharpshooting as well as employ the fieldcraft, stealth and fortitude of the accomplished sniper in both offensive and defensive situations.

To that end, says Pegler, 'The Russians claimed that by 1938 six million soldiers had qualified for the "Voroshiloff Sharpshooter" badge. This is not to say that these men were true snipers, but they were trained riflemen who gave the Russian command a very deep pool when it came to selecting snipers. Some indication of how seriously the Soviet High Command took sniping is the fact that over 53,000 Moisin-Nagant sniping rifles were manufactured up to 1938; by 1942 the same number were being manufactured *annually*.'

Right: *Many female snipers were recruited into the Red Army. Here, Maria Lalkova, who fought for the Czechoslovak army in exile, poses with a Tokarev SVT40 automatic rifle. The Tokarev was one of the best small arms of the war, captured versions of which inspired the Germans to produce the Gewehr 43.*

SOVIET FEMALE SNIPERS

During World War II, the Soviets fielded up to 2000 trained female snipers. One of these was Lydia Gudovantseva, who survived the war with 76 kills.

'I was scared,' Gudovantseva said of her first contact with the enemy. 'We had no idea what our first engagement would be like, and could we fire at a living man. When I first saw a German in my scope, he was walking boldly. Afterward, I felt sorry for him. I signalled to Sasha, who fired and killed a second German who had come out to get his body.'

Another female sniper, Ludmilla Pavlichenko, was credited as many as 309 kills. Of the 2000 female snipers who saw combat, about 500 were killed.

As early as 1924, the Red Army had established several sniping schools to promote accurate shooting. Authors Lester W. Grau and Charles Q. Cutshaw wrote for *Infantry Magazine*, 'At the start of the war, there were two types of Russian snipers – snipers who were part of the Reserves of the Supreme High Command (RVGK) and snipers who were part of the standard infantry units. The RVGK snipers were organized into separate brigades – such as the RVGK sniper brigade made up of women. Entire platoons, companies, and even battalions of RVGK snipers were assigned to fronts and armies to support critical sectors. Snipers were also an important element of TO&E (Table of Operations and Equipment) infantry combat power during World War II, particularly on static battlefields such as Stalingrad. Divisions began the war with a squad of TO&E snipers but expanded their numbers with division sniper schools during the war. By war's end, there were 18 snipers per battalion, or two per rifle platoon.'

'When I first saw a German in my scope, he was walking boldly. Afterward, I felt sorry for him.'

Soviet sniper Lydia Gudovantseva

WEAPONS AND TACTICS

During the 1930s, the Soviet Union had also purchased the Zeiss Optical Company, which produced thousands of optical sights prior to the war. The favoured weapon of most Soviet snipers during World War II was the standard-issue Moisin Nagant 1891/30 rifle enhanced with telescopic sights. In 1938 and 1940, attempts were made to augment the sniper's firepower with the introduction of semi-automatic Tokarev rifles, but these were subsequently withdrawn from service. Along with their sniper rifles, some snipers carried the 7.62mm (0.30in) PPSh submachine gun for close-quarter fighting.

Following Red Army doctrine, snipers regularly hunted in pairs and were deployed to the lowest tactical levels. Junior officers were required to be knowledgeable in their use on the battlefield. They became an integral component of battlefield operations. Regarding numbers of kills, the claims of some Soviet snipers appear astounding. In addition to Zaitsev, other Red Army snipers were said to have dispatched hundreds of Nazi soldiers. A few of these are Ivan Sidorenko, 500; Nikolai Ilyin, 496; (first name unknown) Kulbertinov, 487; Mikhail Budenkov, 437; Fyodor Okhlopkov, 429; and Fyodor Djachenko, 425.

It appears likely that some of these totals were as much the work of propagandist embellishment as they were snipers on the battlefield. The emergence of the 'cult of the sniper' was a phenomenon which developed in Stalinist Russia between the world wars. With the beginning of the Great Patriotic War, as the second conflict was known in the Soviet Union, potential grist for the public relations mill was already budding. In his post-war treatise *With British Snipers To The Reich*, Captain Clifford Shore, himself a former sniper, was virtually incredulous as to the claims.

In a section of his book titled 'Russian Sniping ... and the Great Myth!' Shore states, 'Many fantastic stories have come out of the Slav mists which envelop the U.S.S.R. but none more grotesque than the extraordinary fables of Russian snipers and sniping.'

'I do not think there was any subject about which there was so much balderdash printed and published during the whole course of World War II than Russian sniping,' Shore continued. 'If we are to believe every report we read about the terrific casualties inflicted on the Germans by the Russian *snipers* it was amazing that there were so many Germans left to face the Americans and British in N.W. Europe! ...

LUCKY ESCAPE

Karl-Heinz Pollmann, a German *Fallschirmjäger* (paratrooper) survived three years of combat on the Eastern Front. He was wounded twice. 'On 21st August 1944, I was lying prone behind my MG34, ready to reload,' he remembered, 'when an explosive bullet, fired by a Russian sniper, hit me in the left arm. Dazed with shock, I felt no pain and stared at the wound from which a bubbly trickle of blood was flowing. I swooned. When I came to, I was lying on a garden gate, which three of my comrades were using as a makeshift stretcher to take me to safety.'

'I have met some Russians who had been Red Army men, and saw them shoot in the summer of 1945. If their shooting prowess be taken as a criterion I think that the printed Russian figures of sniper casualties should be divided by a hundred ...

'The *real* sharpshooters of the Russian Army were much respected. But these were not the tommy-gun artisans so beloved of the war correspondents and the Russian information bureaus ...'

Acknowledging the high probability of exaggerated kill totals, an objective student must still accede that Red Army snipers did real damage to the German Army on the Eastern Front in World War II. It may safely be concluded that they did account for a substantial number of German casualties, including many officers. Snipers were lionized in the state-controlled Soviet press, and those who achieved 40 kills against the Germans were decorated with a medal 'for bravery' and given the title of 'noble sniper'. Communist propagandists used these successes and embellished them for public consumption. This tactic was probably successful in its purpose – to steel the resolve of the Soviet people to fight a brutal, protracted war against a determined, ruthless enemy and win the ultimate victory.

GERMAN SNIPERS

The German Army and the *Waffen SS* fielded increasing numbers of snipers on the Eastern Front as combat operations wore on. This was partially in response to the need to counter the successes of the Soviets. In 1967, Captain Hans Widhofer of the Austrian Army interviewed three German snipers who had served in the East. His story appeared in the military magazine *Truppendienst*. The three German veterans had been members of the 3rd Mountain Division. Two of them, Matthias Hetzenauer and Sepp Allerberger, were the top German snipers of the war with 345 and 257 kills respectively. The third was Helmut Wirnsberger, who ended the war with 64.

All three snipers used the standard Mauser-designed K98 rifle with telescopic sights, while Hetzenauer and Wirnsberger also used the semiautomatic G43 and Allerberger employed a captured Soviet model for a time. Hetzenauer asserted that he could hit a standing man from a distance of 700 to 800m (765 to 874 yards).

Below: *Working in tandem, a German sniper armed with a telescopically sighted Karabiner 98K rifle and his observer, looking through binoculars, scour the horizon for Red Army soldiers.*

When asked the range of the furthest target he had fired at during the war, Hetzenauer replied, 'About 1000 meters [1093 yards] … standing soldier. Positive hitting was not possible, but necessary under the circumstances in order to show the enemy that he was not safe even at that distance.'

The three German snipers revealed that they had been part of a battalion sniper group, which numbered as many as 22 men and was commanded by Wirnsberger, and always operated in pairs. Other soldiers within the battalion, they explained, were given rifles with telescopic sights. While these soldiers functioned as members of the rank and file, they were also assigned some tasks which might have been given to more highly trained snipers.

In response to a question about target priorities, the three agreed. 'Elimination of observers, of the enemy's heavy weapons and of commanders, or special order when all important or worthwhile targets were eliminated, for example, anti-tank gun positions, machine gun positions, and so on. Snipers followed closely the attacking units and whenever necessary eliminated enemies who operated heavy weapons and those who were dangerous to our advance.'

Below: *A German soldier scans enemy lines through the scope of his Karabiner 98 sniper rifle, Belorussia 1943.*

KARABINER 98K

Country of Origin	Germany
Calibre	7.92mm (0.31in)
Overall length	1250mm (49in)
Barrel length	740mm (29.1in)
Weight	3.9kg (8.6lb)

Hetzenauer noted, 'In a few cases, I had to penetrate the enemy's main line of resistance at night before our own attack. When our own artillery had opened fire, I had to shoot at enemy commanders and gunners because our own forces would have been too weak in number and ammunition without this support.'

The Germans also related that they used appropriate camouflage where necessary, including Allerberger's employment of a fan or 'umbrella' painted to resemble the terrain. Using tactics reminiscent of some seen on the Western Front during World War I, Hetzenauer and Allerberger deployed dummies, some of which included rifles fired remotely by pulling a wire, to draw fire from enemy snipers.

SIEGE CONDITIONS

During the epic 900-day siege of Leningrad (now once more St Petersburg), the city's civilian population suffered perhaps as no other in history. The sniper also found himself in static, trench-line conditions similar to those of the Western Front in World War I. In his 1951 book *Dance Of Death*, author Erich Kern recalled visiting German snipers at the strategically vital Narva bridgehead near the besieged city.

'We were lying hard up against the enemy, in places no more than [43.7m] forty yards from their lines,' Kern wrote. 'It was a sniper's war. Dead silence reigned in the narrow strip of shell-torn land between us and the Soviet sap. Occasionally a heavy shell rumbled across the lines, and occasionally we heard the swish of the "Hitler Scythe", as the Russians called our machine guns.

'Then silence, heavy and oppressive, dropped again over the spectral landscape. Rain fell in a steady monotony out of a pale grey sky. Water stood knee-high in the trenches and gurgled over the edge of our gumboots.

'Undeterred by the weather, men stood here and there in the trenches gazing motionless towards the Russian line, sometimes alone, sometimes in pairs, one with the periscope, and the other resting to save his strength for the strike.

'A boy's eyes gazed hard and cool towards the enemy trench. From the corner of his mouth came a whisper: "Nothing doing here". Two men who were walking, bent and stooping, along the trench towards us, straightened a little as they passed and in the same moment a sharp report rent the sodden air like the crack of a whip. We ducked. Who wanted to die in the dreary grey of a wet morning? Again the deathlike silence came down and we went on our way. But the sniper in the front line at Narva stood motionless, gazing into the coming day.

'We met more of them farther along the line, this time two boys from the Siebenburgen, Rudolf aged nineteen and Michael aged twenty-four. We talked to them about their homes, about the war, about everything. Rudolf's father was a huntsman, his brother a huntsman, and he had it in his blood. Put a gun in his hand and his eye looked for a target. Michael had seen his first hunt while still a boy. Now they were back at the butts, but here the quarry fired back. "We must only fire occasionally and we have to hit them when we do", Rudolf said, his eyes alight, "otherwise we give ourselves away".

'A Red Army man showed himself in the opposite trench. A quick aim, then "Crack!" and he fell forward. A hit? – or had he merely ducked for cover? More hours of waiting and then at last a target. Another shot. The man on the other side stopped and tilted backwards. A pencil mark on the stockade – that one counted. I asked what they thought about as they stood there crossing them off one after another. "Only that there's one more gone; one less to hold a rifle", they said.

'Sometimes the "opposite number" across the way spotted one of our snipers. Where was he? Once the target was sighted, a duel developed in which every conceivable trick was used, every scrap of cunning. A whole magazine might be fired off from a feint position, then a quick dash back to the old stand to see if the enemy would reply. Once the position was located it was usually the end of the duel. Sometimes it was our man who lost. Then another took his place as the eyes of the forward line, behind those whose vigilance the others could afford to relax.'

TOTAL WAR

Often, a fleeting, unguarded moment meant opportunity for the sniper on the Eastern Front. While the prospect of a sniper's bullet kept soldiers on edge a great deal of the time, some seemed to find the constant, gnawing concern overwhelming, as death became a common occurrence and was considered

Below: With comrades in a trench to the rear and goggles affixed to his helmet, a soldier of the SS Death's Head Division scans the Ukrainian steppes through his telescopic sight, seeking out easy targets.

almost routine. In *Frontsoldaten: The German Soldier in World War II*, author Stephen G. Fritz recounted a few lines in a letter home from soldier Harry Mielert.

'I stood immediately next to him [Captain O.], about 150 meters [164 yards] opposite an undergrowth in which Russian sharpshooters lay. He was hit, I had the luck instantly to have thrown myself down … as soon as I saw the fellow lying there before us. The captain reacted a fraction of a second later and was wounded.'

Urban warfare presented special hazards for troops advancing into the killing zones of snipers. Every window, heap of rubble or immobilized vehicle might harbour a skilled rifleman. Conversely, a sniper in the close confines of a building or a city street might have even less time to target and fire before his position was compromised and roles were reversed. Tragically, amid the cruelty of total war, the sniper might also turn his attention to the civilian population. Such was one poignant case as told by author William Craig in his landmark 1973 book *Enemy At The Gates: The Battle For Stalingrad*.

Above: *A squad of Red Army soldiers inches through the rubble of Berlin, April 1945, to root out snipers in the German capital. Counter-sniper operations often proved extremely hazardous in heavily built-up areas.*

79

'They ran into the street and fell into a zig-zag trench beside Russian soldiers and civilians. A little girl lay huddled up, her body punctured with shrapnel. She screamed and screamed: "Find my mama before I die."

'Mrs. Karmanova could not bear it. As she crouched under a hail of bullets and tried to block out the sounds of the dying child, she saw a family dart from shelter and run toward the river. At the same moment, a German sniper tracked them and quickly killed the son, the father, and then the mother. The sole survivor, a little girl, paused in bewilderment over her mother's body. In the trench, Russian soldiers cupped their hands and hollered, "Run! Run!" Others took up the cry. The girl hesitated, then bolted from the corpses into the darkness. The German sniper did not fire again.'

Undoubtedly, the snipers of both the Red Army and the *Wehrmacht* influenced the conduct of World War II on the Eastern Front. On the open steppes or in the confines of an urban combat zone, snipers duelled with one another, exacted a toll on the enemy and gathered vital information.

The war in the East between the Soviet Union and Nazi Germany was the bloodiest in human history. An estimated 20 million Soviet military personnel and civilians died in the four-year conflict. From the crucible of the Great Patriotic War, a new order emerged in Eastern Europe, and the sniper truly became a figure of legendary proportions.

ZAITSEV'S 'STUDENTS'

During the battle for Stalingrad, soldiers were continually trained in the most basic elements of sniping. One such 'school' was the huge, cavernous Lazur chemical plant. According to author William Craig, instructors conducted a short but intense course on sniping there while the battle for the city raged around them. At one end of a makeshift rifle range the instructors stood with their charges, who fired at a distant wall on which helmets, human torsos and observation slits had been painted. The graduates left the Lazur plant and immediately entered the fray.

One of Zaitsev's students was Tania Chernova, a young woman of Russian-American heritage, who was also reported to have been his lover. The Nazis had murdered Tania's grandparents, and she waged a personal war of vengeance. Craig wrote of an incident which led to severe repercussions for her.

'Further south near the Red October Plant, sniper Vassili Zaitsev stalked the front lines. By now he had killed nearly a hundred Germans and had been decorated with the Order of Lenin. His fame was spreading to all parts of the Soviet Union.

'Furthermore, his students had amassed a formidable number of victims. Men like Viktor Medvedev and Anatoli Chekhov made the Germans afraid to lift their heads during daylight hours. And sharpshooter Tania Chernova now fired a rifle with unerring accuracy. Almost forty Germans had died in her sights, victims she continued to refer to as "sticks". But Tania still had much to learn.

'In the top story of a building, she settled down behind piles of bricks to monitor enemy traffic. Several other student snipers joined her as she waited for hours, tracking Germans who scurried back and forth between trenches. Tania and her squad followed each one with scopes zeroed in on heads and hearts. But no one fired, because Zaitsev had told them to wait for his approval before revealing their position.

'Tania seethed at the order. Filled with disgust at having lost so many "sticks", she fidgeted at the window and cursed the delay. When a column of German infantrymen suddenly burst into the open, she screamed: "Shoot!" and the room blazed with gunfire. Tania pumped shot after shot into the gray green uniforms and counted seventeen dead men sprawled on the pavement. Exultant, she sat back and exchanged congratulations with her friends.

'But they had missed some Germans, who crawled back to their lines with exact coordinates of Tania's ambush. In minutes, a succession of shellbursts blew the building in on the Russians. Tania left the dead and ran out to tell Vassili Zaitsev what had happened.

'When he heard the distraught girl's story, Zaitsev slapped her across the face with all his strength, berated her for her stupidity, and told her that she alone was responsible for the deaths of her friends. Stricken with guilt and afraid of Zaitsev's wrath, Tania cried for hours.'

Sometime later, Chernova, who was also called the 'blond sniper', was seriously wounded by an exploding land mine. She was reported to have killed 80 Germans during only three months of fighting in the vicinity of Stalingrad. She believed that Vassili Zaitsev had been killed but was astonished to learn nearly 30 years after the war that he was still alive. The master sniper had been decorated as a Hero of the Soviet Union and become the head of an engineering school in Kiev. He died quietly in 1992.

Following an encounter with Japanese forces on Guadalcanal in November 1942, a US Marine shows a comrade the camouflage jacket once worn by an enemy sniper who faced his unit. The fighting on Guadalcanal lasted nearly six months and resulted in heavy casualties on both sides before the Americans secured the island in February 1943.

CHAPTER FIVE

THE PACIFIC THEATRE

On uninhabited islands and in steaming jungles, Allied troops battled a resourceful enemy in the Japanese soldier, who was willing to die and asked no quarter. The snipers of both sides took a heavy toll during four years of desperate combat.

Bushido, the ancient warrior code, dictated the life and sanctified the death of the Japanese soldier during World War II. Steeped in the tradition of the samurai, he was inculcated with the belief that death in battle, giving his life for the emperor, was the most noble of sacrifices. A tenacious and dedicated foe, the Japanese soldier was a master of camouflage, a willing taker of great risk and in many cases a seasoned veteran of jungle warfare. As conquerors and later defenders of a vast area stretching from the frontier of India to the tropical islands of the Pacific, Japanese troops regularly fought to the death. Only a relative handful were taken prisoner during World War II, for such a fate was considered worse than death, dishonourable to the soldier and to his family.

The willing self-sacrifice of the Japanese soldier made him a doubly difficult adversary when employed in the sniper role. Often, a sniper would lie in wait, even allowing Allied troops to pass him by, and open fire from behind as he popped from a spider hole or aimed from his nearly invisible perch in a coconut tree. He was armed initially with the 6.5mm (0.25in) calibre Arisaka Type 38 rifle, and later with the 6.5mm (0.25in) calibre Type 97 and 7.7mm (0.303in) calibre Type 99 fitted with telescopic sights; he would sometimes even employ a Nambu light machine gun. The reduced visibility and close confines of the jungle often limited the incidences of snipers firing from great distances during the Pacific War. Nevertheless, the toughness and endurance of the Japanese sniper earned grudging respect from those who faced him.

In *Sniper*, author Adrian Gilbert describes a favoured tactic of Japanese snipers, which inflicted many casualties and effectively harassed Allied troops throughout the war in the Pacific. 'A distinctive feature of Japanese sniping was the use of trees as firing platforms. In some cases small tree chairs would be hauled up into the higher branches; in others the sniper would be tied into position, which prevented him falling out of the tree if shot,

TYPE 99

Country of Origin	Japan
Calibre	6.5mm (0.25in)
Overall length	1275mm (50.2in)
Barrel length	797mm (31.4in)
Weight	4.2kg (9.25lb)

thus informing the countersniper team that they had scored a hit. As an aid to clambering up and down the trees, the sniper was issued with climbing spikes. To Allied and German snipers the use of trees was discouraged (although observers used them regularly, and were often mistaken for snipers) because they became a death trap if the sniper was discovered.'

Generally, the Japanese sniper worked alone, using a thin netting to camouflage his face and a cape adorned with palm fronds and foliage to break up his silhouette. In addition to the spikes, he was equipped with shoes with separate fittings for the big toe to assist in climbing trees. Often, as British, Australian and American soldiers discovered as the war progressed, the Japanese notched trees to ease the climb and even placed rifles in the treetops along with the most basic of supplies so that the higher elevation position could be occupied quickly.

Neutralizing enemy snipers proved a daunting task for Allied soldiers, with the progress of entire formations of troops sometimes being held up for hours. Gilbert notes mention of Japanese sniping proficiency in the New Guinea jungle as told in the history of the US 41st Infantry Division.

'From a tree almost anywhere around our oval perimeter, a Jap sharpshooter could choose a Yank target who had to leave his water-soaked hole. The range could be all of [183–366m] 200–400 yards. The keen-eyed sniper could steady his precision killing tool on a branch and tighten the butt to his shoulder. He could take a clear sight picture and squeeze the trigger. All 1/Bn might hear is a Jap [6.5mm] .25-calibre cartridge crack, like a Fourth of July cap sparked on a stone. Then a Yank cowering in a hole might hear the prolonged dying groan of a man in his next squad. Or long after a deadly silence, he might find his buddy a pale corpse with a deceptively small hole in his forehead.'

Adding to the difficulty of spotting Japanese snipers was the fact that the relatively small charge of powder in the 6.5mm (0.25in) rifle cartridge and the long barrel of the rifle itself meant that little telltale smoke would be apparent to mark the sniper's hiding place. Firing indiscriminately into treetops with the powerful Browning Automatic Rifle (BAR) might be the most efficient and effective method of dealing with a troublesome sniper. Even then, there were delays and the virtually inevitable cost in lives associated with the encounter.

In the early days of the Pacific War, American forces were desperate to strike a blow against the Japanese. In a hit-and-run raid against enemy-held Makin atoll in the Gilbert Islands during the summer of 1942, US Marine raiders lost 19 killed. One of these, Captain Gerald Holtom, the only officer to die during the raid, was shot by a sniper. The marching orders for the Japanese sniper were similar to those of other military organizations around the globe. Their primary responsibility was to neutralize enemy officers or to engage enemy snipers. This was followed by attacking the crews of heavier weapons such as mortars and machine guns. Because he usually fought to the death, intelligence-gathering responsibilities were less significant.

GUADALCANAL

The first major ground offensive by US troops in the Pacific began in August 1942 as Marines slogged ashore on the island of Guadalcanal in the Solomons archipelago. Richard Tregaskis was with the Marines and penned his classic *Guadalcanal Diary*, which includes more than one close call with Japanese snipers.

Below: *Cautiously probing the jungle on Guadalcanal, Marines search the treetops for Japanese snipers, August 1942. The initial landings on the island faced only light opposition.*

'More Jap .25s [6.5mm rifles] opened up ahead; a storm of fire broke and filled the jungle. I dived for the nearest tree, which unfortunately stood somewhat alone and was not surrounded by deep foliage. While the firing continued and I could hear the occasional impact of a bullet hitting a nearby tree or snapping off a twig, I debated whether it would be wiser to stay in my exposed spot or to run for a better 'ole and risk being hit by a sniper en route.

'I was still debating the question when I heard a bullet whirr very close to my left shoulder, heard it thud into the ground and then heard the crack of the rifle which had fired it. That was bad. Two Marines on the ground [3.1 or 4.6m] ten or fifteen feet ahead of me turned and looked to see if I had been hit. They had evidently heard the bullet passing. That made up my mind. I jumped up and made for a big bush. I found it well populated with ants which crawled up my trouser legs, but such annoyances were secondary now.

Below: His helmet covered with netting and foliage for camouflage, a US Marine sniper takes aim through his telescopic-sighted Springfield Model 1903 rifle on the island of New Georgia in the Solomons.

'The sniper who had fired at me was still on my track. He had evidently spotted my field-glasses and taken me for a regular officer.

'I searched the nearby trees, but could see nothing moving, no smoke, no signs of any sniper. Then a .25 [6.5mm rifle] cracked again and I heard the bullet pass – fortunately not as close as before. I jumped for better cover, behind two close trees which were surrounded by ferns, small pineapple plants and saplings. Here I began to wish I had a rifle. I should like to find that sniper, I thought. I had made an ignominious retreat. My dignity had been offended.'

WEAPONRY

On the eve of US entry into World War II, the standard Army infantry squad included one soldier designated as a sniper, relates author Robert S. Rush in *US Infantryman in World War II (1), Pacific Area of Operations 1941–45*. While the standard issue rifle was the semiautomatic M-1 Garand, the sniper was armed with the proven bolt-action Springfield Model 1903. The Army allocated very few resources to sniper training, and many of those who carried the Springfield were simply the best shot available. The US Marine Corps, on the other hand, placed greater, though often inconsistent, emphasis on sniper training. With the war already underway, sniper programmes were begun in late 1942 and early 1943 at Camp LeJeune, North Carolina, and Green's Farm near San Diego, California, respectively.

'The school at Green's Farm,' writes Gilbert, 'came under the command of Lieutenant Claude N. Harris, a noted marksman and winner of the 1935 National Rifle Championship. Harris ran a series of five-week courses, where fifteen-strong teams were instructed in a broad-based syllabus which included marksmanship, camouflage, observation and fieldcraft, map reading, military sketching and the interpretation of aerial photographs. This reflected the Marine belief that the sniper should be capable of fulfilling a reconnaissance role, hence their official title of "scout snipers". After graduation they were allotted to field units, three to each company; two would form the usual sniper-spotter team while the third man would act as a reserve in case of casualties or illness.'

NEW GUINEA AND PELELIU

The Japanese military did utilize the sniper in a limited offensive role; however, his ability to control movement through the jungle or across the sands of a tropical atoll proved most effective in defence. Eliminating the snipers in their path was an

HUNTER IS THE HUNTED

On another occasion, Richard Tregaskis became a target once again:

'Suddenly I saw the foliage move in a tree across the valley. I looked again and was astonished to see the figure of a man in the crotch of the tree. He seemed to be moving his arms and upper body. I was so amazed at seeing him so clearly that I might have sat there and reflected on the matter if my reflexes had not been functioning – which they fortunately were. I flopped flat on the ground just as I heard the sniper's gun go off and the bullet whirred over my head. I knew then that his movement had been the raising of his gun.'

Above: *In the spring of 1942 on the island of New Caledonia, an Australian sniper of the Third Landing Group demonstrates the effectiveness of cover and concealment.*

arduous task for Allied soldiers. In his *Brief History Of The 6th Infantry Division*, Thomas E. Price recounted the formation's initial landings at Milne Bay, New Guinea. 'The Division set up camp near the Australian forces in a place that was a palm tree plantation owned by the Palmolive Palm Oil Company. The men were told that they would be fined if they cut down the trees. The first Japanese shot was wearing an American uniform. He was assumed to have been a scout or a spy. A 6th Division medic shot him. There were problems with Japanese snipers in the trees at Milne Bay. The trees came down, or their crowns were cropped and pruned with machine guns. There was no more talk of fines for trees.'

Like his predecessors in earlier conflicts, small groups of Japanese snipers were capable of sowing confusion and demoralizing large numbers of troops, many times the strength of a single skilled marksman. In his book *The Devil's Anvil*, James H. Hallas described the hardship and heroism exhibited during the bitter fight for the island of Peleliu 804km (500 miles) east of the Philippines.

'For the individual riflemen, the push was one prolonged horror. Private Russell Davis was hunkered down by a causeway over a swamp beneath the ridges when a Marine dashing toward the hills was shot to a skidding stop. As the man lay there in the open just beyond reach, his muddy hand opened and closed, whether in pain or in the reflex of death, Davis did not know.

'Another Marine, unable to bear the sight, clambered up on the causeway to help the man. A bullet knocked him on his back, where he lay without a twitch. "Shove this", blurted a corpsman. "I'm gonna get those guys." He managed to get to his knees before a sniper shot him. Finally, a burly Marine reached up over the edge of the causeway and, grunting and sweating with effort, managed to pull all three wounded men to shelter.'

'DEAD MAN'S CURVE'

The highest ranking casualty of the 1st Marine Division on the island of Peleliu was Colonel Joseph F. Hankins, commander of the division headquarters battalion, who was shot by a sniper on 3 October 1944.

'For the previous day or two, Japanese snipers had worked their way into the high ground dominating a section of the road – promptly dubbed "Dead Man's Curve" – less than [1829m] 2000 yards north of the airfield, where they began harassing traffic from the cave-pocked cliff face,' wrote Hallas. 'On the afternoon of 3 October, Hankins, a member of several famous Marine Corps rifle teams, picked up an M-1 and a pair of binoculars and set out to snipe the snipers. The colonel's plan suffered a setback as soon as he arrived at the ill-famed curve. An LVT and three trucks were jammed up on the road under heavy small-arms fire from the nearby cliff face only [46m] 50 yards away. The men had deserted the vehicles to find cover, leaving the road blocked.

'Unmindful of the enemy fire, Hankins strode to the middle of the road to restore order. He had just gotten the crews back on their vehicles when a bullet thwacked into his chest, killing him ...

'Following Hankins's death, a Marine company was sent into the area to clean up the high ground near Dead Man's Curve. They managed to put a temporary halt to the sniping, but it later became necessary to place three medium tanks at the curve. The crews blasted the cliffs whenever snipers became bothersome, which was frequently.'

When the Americans moved artillery into another hotly contested area on Peleliu, the initial results were successful, Hallas related. 'The fire "routed out a covey of Nips", reported [Lieutenant Colonel Edson A.] Lyman. About a dozen Japanese were seen jumping and sliding off the eastern side of the hill to escape the shelling. Soon after, the gun crew was taken under heavy small-arms fire from a distance of only [68.6m] 75 yards.

'The Marine crew kept shooting, but by the time it had fired 40 rounds, one man had been hit, and as Lyman noted, "it was deemed expedient to secure." Two more Marines were picked off at daybreak – shot through the head by Japanese snipers from just across the canyon – and it was decided to halt further artillery operations from the position.'

Once American troops fought their way off the beaches, they were confronted many times with islands whose inland areas were honeycombed with caves, dotted with hills, criss-crossed by fetid swamps and stagnant streams, and scarred by ridges, ravines and sheer cliffs. Although Peleliu was thought to be well defended, it was hoped that the Marines could wrest control of the island in a few days. In reality, over 10,000 Japanese soldiers, resigned to their fate, defended the island to the end. The fighting lasted more than two months.

All too quickly, it became apparent to the American fighting man that his stealthy Japanese opponent was nothing like the stereotypical comic version with thick glasses and buck teeth, who was the subject of disdain back home. The pervasive fear of being caught in a sniper's sights was capable of sapping individual strength and unit morale. One incident reported on Peleliu ended with the deaths of Army Tech 5 Philip Griego and a Japanese sniper. Griego, a cook who had volunteered to fill the depleted ranks of a rifle squad, spotted the sniper at the same time he became a target himself. Both men fired, and each shot was accurate.

IWO JIMA – THE HARSH REALITIES OF COMBAT

During the spring of 1945, Pharmacist's Mate 2nd Class Fred P. Brinkman of the U.S. Navy wrote a letter home describing the shock and unpredictability of war while serving on the volcanic island of Iwo Jima. A member of a beach party that came ashore from the transport USS *Lowndes* a day after the initial assault, Brinkman and other medical personnel were tending injured Marines when a comrade suddenly became a casualty.

'Just after noon, things got hotter than ever before,' Brinkman told his family. 'Just behind us was a battered Jap pillbox which had been smashed in. But a Jap sniper poked his head out of a hole and opened up ... Don Bowman was only a few feet away giving plasma to a wounded Marine. Don never knew what happened ... He fell against me and knocked me down ... Of course, the Nip didn't last long ... I grabbed my carbine, and even though about ten other guys must have hit him first, I kept my finger on that trigger until my ammunition clip was empty. After we had ceased firing, I was so mad, I jammed the butt of my rifle into his face as hard as I could.'

MARINE SNIPERS

While they were employed in the anticipated sniping role when possible, Marine snipers in the Pacific usually operated in pairs as counter-snipers providing perimeter protection and some degree of suppressive fire. As the scout-sniper role evolved during World War II, these troops developed an *esprit de corps* which was unmistakable. Their training was rigorous, and often their leadership was courageous almost beyond belief. On 20 November 1943, the Marines hit the beach on Betio, the primary islet of an atoll in the Gilbert Islands known as Tarawa. Young Lieutenant William Deane Hawkins led the Scout-Sniper Platoon to Betio's shore five minutes ahead of the first wave. Fighting at platoon strength was uncharacteristic of the scout-snipers, but their value was about to become apparent.

In *Strong Men Armed*, author Robert Leckie wrote of the scout-sniper effort at Tarawa, for which Hawkins was award a posthumous Congressional Medal of

Honor. 'Hawkins and the Scout-Snipers went in to seize the pier extending about [457m] 500 yards into the lagoon. It split the landing beaches, and from it numerous Japanese latrines now filled with riflemen and machine gunners could rake the marine amtracs passing either side.

'Hawkins had his men in two landing boats, one commanded by himself, the other by Gunnery Sgt. Jared Hooper. In a third boat were the flame-throwing engineers of Lt. Alan Leslie.

'They came in and hit the reef. They were held up there, just as enemy mortars began to drop among them and drums of gasoline, stacked on the pier, began to burn. Sniper and machine-gun fire raked the boats. Airplanes were called down on the enemy guns while Hawkins and his men awaited transfer to amtracs. They got them and rode in to assault the pier. They fought with flamethrowers, with grenades, with bayonets. They fought yard by yard, killing and being killed, while the pier still burned, and swept ashore to attack enemy pillboxes.

'Like Hector in his chariot, Lieutenant Hawkins stood erect in his amtrac as it butted through barbed wire, climbed the seawall and clanked among the enemy spitting fire and grenades.'

The following day, Hawkins was ordered to destroy a Japanese strongpoint housing five machine guns. 'Hawk gathered his men,' Leckie continued. 'He had often said,

Above: *A US soldier test fires an experimental .30in (7.62mm) calibre Model 45-A rifle fitted with a telescopic sight in the recently liberated city of Manila, Philippines, October 1945.*

Above: *Stripped of his clothing, one of the relatively few Japanese soldiers captured alive sits under guard during the Marshall Islands campaign in February 1944. More often than not Japanese soldiers would fight to the death.*

"I think my thirty-four-man platoon can lick any two-hundred-man company in the world." Now he was going on a company-size mission to prove it. His men moved methodically from gun to gun, laying down covering fire while Hawkins crawled up to the pillbox gunports to fire point-blank inside or toss in grenades. The guns fell, but not before Hawkins had been shot in the chest. He had already lost blood from shrapnel wounds the day before, but he still resisted the corpsman's suggestions that he accept evacuation.'

A short time later, Lieutenant Hawkins was mortally wounded by an exploding shell. He was carried to the rear and later buried at the Punchbowl Cemetery in Honolulu, Hawaii.

SAIPAN

While the D-Day invasion was taking place in Europe in June 1944, a bitter battle was being waged for control of the island of Saipan in the Marianas. Saipan and its sister islands Guam and Tinian were strategically vital to the US island-hopping offensive against the Japanese. These Pacific outposts and their airfields would bring the cities of Japan within range of the huge Boeing B-29 Superfortress bombers which could rain destruction on the enemy. When Marine snipers did function in their more conventional role, they could be called upon to eliminate pockets of Japanese resistance which might pin down units along their route of advance. They were employed successfully on a number of occasions at Saipan.

'We were pinned down on the beach at Saipan by a machine-gun bunker,' one Marine recounted in Gilbert's *Stalk and Kill – The Sniper Experience.* 'The pill-box commanded a sweeping view of the area, and there was just no way we could get at it. Plenty of our boys had died trying.

'Finally one of our ninety-day wonders [an inexperienced officer] got on the horn and requested a sniper. A few minutes later, I saw two old gunnery sergeants sashaying towards us, wearing shooting jackets and campaign hats! As soon as I saw these Smokey Bears bobbing over to us, I figured this could be some show. And it was.

'These two old sergeants skinnied up to the lieutenant and just asked him to point out the bunker. Then they unfolded two shooting mats, took off their Smokey Bears and settled down to business. One manned a spotter's scope while the other fired a 1903 Springfield with a telescopic sight rig.

'That bunker must have been [1006–1097m] 1100 or 1200 yards away, but in just a few minutes, with three or four spotting rounds, this old gunny on the Springfield slipped a round right into the bunker's firing slit. One dead machine-gunner. But their commander just stuck another man on that gun. Our sniper shot him, too. After the fourth man bit a slug, I think they got the idea. We moved up on their flank and destroyed the bunker while our snipers kept the machine-gun silent. Then the two gunnys dusted themselves off, rolled up their mats and settled their Smokey Bears back on their heads. And just moseyed away.'

OKINAWA

On 1 April 1945, the final land battle of the Pacific War commenced with the invasion of Okinawa, a mere 531km (330 miles) southwest of the Japanese home islands. The defenders did not contest the initial American landings on the Okinawan beaches, but an elaborate network of defences exacted a heavy toll during the effort to secure the southern portion of the island.

In *One Shot – One Kill*, Charles W. Sasser and Craig Roberts present the story of Marine Private Daniel W. Cass, who performed one of the more remarkable feats of marksmanship during the entire war.

'A tired sniper might risk a try at one of the sweaty, broad backs lying below him, but he's a punk shot. If he tries to fire more than once every hour, he is quickly spotted and cut into quarters …'

Author Stanley Frankel

'Carter cast me a glance as he slung his 20X spotting scope on a strap across his back and gave his Thompson .45 a quick check to make sure it wasn't plugged with mud. I stuck a .38 revolver in my pocket and led the way forward with my '03. Panting from exertion, we found our way to the top of a ridge overlooking the valley, all the time listening to the intermittent chatter of the Nambu as it grew louder the closer we got …

Right: *American soldiers view the bodies of three Japanese snipers lying in a bomb crater. The Japanese were killed by an artillery barrage on the Philippine island of Leyte. The Americans often employed heavy weapons and artillery as an effective means of rooting out snipers.*

'Marines scurried among a field of shell craters and shattered forest; they sprawled motionless behind whatever cover they could find. A few of them lay in the open. They were dead. Nips high on the ridge opposite from us sprayed them with a deadly hail of lead …

'At least [1097m] 1200 yards of valley separated us from the machine gun nests. Fog made for such poor visibility that I could not tell where the firing came from. Desperately, I used my rifle scope to search for gun smoke or some movements to give the Japs away. Carter used his spotting scope. I saw caves and coral ledges and ragged stumps. Down in the valley a Marine jumped up to improve his position. An invisible finger fell out of the air and seemed to flip off his head. The body went tumbling and flopping …

'Carter spoke first: "I found them."

> ## 'THE LADY SNIPER FROM TOKYO' (ANON. MARINE)
>
> 'Gather 'round chillun; keep quite still;
> Listen to the legend of Bougainville.
> Hear about the lady with the two gun style,
> Who shot em down dead for over a mile.
> Amazing, amusing, Tokyo Sal,
> I never saw her, but I have a pal,
> Who knows a guy who heard it's true,
> She doesn't shape up like our girls do …
> A sad tale comes from a friend of a friend
> Of a dope who got his reward in the end,
> He wouldn't take cover; he chanced a glance
> at Sal, and she plugged him right in the pants …
> She shot down troops in the rear CPs
> And lured on more with a burlesque tease.
> Camouflage made her a great success,
> As Chaplain she ate in the General's mess….'

'I followed his point to a spot located just below a coral ledge honeycombed with shallow caves. The nest was well camouflaged and dug in, but I detected a thin screen of smoke coming from what appeared to be toppled underbrush. The smoke was a little bluer than that made by shellfire, and it was darker than the shredded remnants of fog …

'"I estimate [1097 or 1189m] twelve or thirteen hundred yards," Carter said …

'A whole lot of variables entered into shooting at a range of even [914m] one thousand yards, the longest shot I had ever tried. Wind and heat waves and, in this case, fog distorted the scope picture …

'Smoke curled up from behind the logs as the Nambu commenced to chatter its short repetitive phrases.

'Deep breath. Let half out. Hold. Cross-hair, cross-hair, squeeze …

'Carter grunted. "All right", he said when my first round plunged into the enemy's barricade …

'I worked the bolt with a feeling of elation. My hands and breathing were surprisingly steady. I fired and worked the bolt, fired and worked the bolt, pouring accurate fire into the Japanese defences, cross-hairing handkerchief-sized targets momentarily exposed more than a half mile away. Even through his spotting scope, Carter couldn't tell when I scored because the targets were so fleeting they disappeared whether I made a hit or not, but he was all grins.

'The machine gun fire ceased.'

The British and Australian troops battling the Japanese on the Asian mainland adopted tactics to deal with snipers as the war progressed. Gilbert noted that an official report confirmed the tally of a 48-man British sniper brigade to be 296 Japanese killed or wounded during a period of only two weeks. A former kangaroo hunter on the island of Timor was reported to have shot 47 Japanese soldiers.

If nothing else, the Japanese sniper was persistent and willing to engage the enemy with incredible disregard for his own safety. Pharmacists Mate 2nd Class Frank R. Viglas was a member of the Third Medical Detachment attached to the 3rd Marines on the island of Bougainville. In his diary, Viglas made numerous references to the presence of snipers, illustrating the fact that the possibility of a quick death from a single bullet was constant.

'Nip [Japanese] snipers picking at us from the nearest island,' Viglas wrote. 'No one got hurt. Finally Raiders cleaned off snipers and we unloaded supplies. Seabees are busy already cutting a trail through the swamp with two bulldozers. Can hear them cussing at Nip snipers ...

'Operations and plaster casts all morning ... Shock cases pouring in ... One corpsman got himself two snipers with his automatic rifle ...

'Couple of sniper victims came in this A.M. picked off just across the road from us. One is pretty bad. Shot through the neck and chest ... Party went out looking for those snipers that have been firing at us at the creek. They had no luck ... Our serious sniper victim died on us tonight at about 2230.'

One rumour which circulated through the ranks on Bougainville was of a Japanese female who sniped at the Americans. Whether true or not, this yarn was typical of the scuttlebutt which might make the rounds in a combat zone.

IWO JIMA

The epic battle for the capture of Iwo Jima, a rough island of volcanic rock and black sand, which was dominated by 168m (550ft) Mount Suribachi, began on 19 February 1945, and ended a month later. The fight for this spit of land 1223km (760 miles) from Tokyo was the backdrop for the war's most enduring image, the famous photo by Associated Press photographer Joe Rosenthal depicting the raising of the American flag atop Suribachi.

The importance of Iwo Jima lay in its location, between the B-29 bases in the Marianas and the home islands of Japan. Wounded bombers returning from the massive air raids could find a haven at an emergency airstrip there. The lives of thousands of airmen would be saved with Iwo Jima in American hands; however, in order to secure the island other lives would have to be lost.

Charles Ray Barnes was a 19-year-old member of the 4th Marine Division on Iwo Jima, and he witnessed the ferocity of the Japanese defenders, many of whom had to be buried alive in caves or burned out of bunkers. On 26 February, his

Opposite: A lone US Marine sniper fires at a Japanese pillbox during the battle to capture Tarawa atoll in the Gilbert Islands in November 1943. This artillery-ravaged landscape offers little cover to the sniper.

regiment had participated in the capture of Hill 382. The following day, he saw a machine gun from a neighbouring unit go into action.

'They started shooting at something across there,' Barnes remembered in *Leathernecks on Bloody Iwo Jima*. 'Directly, a sniper got the man on the machine gun. The next man took over and he was shot. Then the third man crawled up to the machine gun and the sniper got him. The sniper shot three of 'em. They hid everywhere. They would come up behind you, in front of you, it didn't seem to make any difference.'

A number of methods were employed to deal with the Japanese sniper menace. When confronted by a sniper, standard infantry tactics of fire and manoeuvre were employed if possible. Exposed soldiers were directed to take cover, and the sniper was located. Suppressive fire was placed on the sniper's position by one group, while another moved left or right and eliminated the sniper from the flank.

Necessity, however, is the mother of invention. Allied troops employed a variety of methods to combat snipers in the Pacific. Gilbert noted that Australian artilleryman Russell Braddon assisted a comrade in the jungle.

'I was amazed to see a fellow gunner raise a heavy Boyes anti-tank rifle to his shoulder, aim high and fire. He was at once flung backwards, whilst the half-inch shell most certainly passed harmlessly into the stratosphere. When I reached him he was rubbing his shattered right shoulder and swearing softly but with that consummate fluency which is the prerogative of the Australian farmer who is perpetually harassed by the cussedness of things inanimate.

'"What the hell are you trying to do, Harry?" I asked.

'"Get that bloody sniper up the top of that bloody tree", he replied tersely. It appeared that, fired off the ground, the Boyes rifle had not sufficient elevation to hit a tree high up. However, since the sniper fired from behind the top of the tree trunk he could only be shot through it – a Boyes rifle was, therefore, essential for the job. We decided to do it together. With the barrel resting on my shoulder, the butt against his

DOGS OF WAR

Everything from rifle to machine gun, the BAR to the hand grenade, and the anti-tank gun to the satchel charge was employed to silence the deadly Japanese sniper. On Peleliu, the 4th War Dog Platoon deployed, and Hallas notes that it reported one of its dogs 'alerted [detected] a Jap sniper at about [45.7m] 50 yards distance and killed him'. The following day a dog by the name of Pardner was reported to have 'chased a Jap sniper approximately [137m] 150 yards before the sniper was killed'. Such events, which might seem extraordinary, became commonplace during the Pacific War and serve as a testament to the tenacity of the Japanese sniper.

Left: *US Marine
Raiders and their
specially trained war
dogs move out on patrol
on the island of
Bougainville, 1943.*

own. Harry took a long aim, apparently quite undeterred by the bursts of bullets from
all sides, which our stance attracted. I was not in the least undeterred. In fact, as we
stood there, our feet spread wide apart to take some of the shock, I was very deterred
indeed. Then Harry fired and I was crushed to the ground and Harry was flung against
a tree and the sniper toppled gracelessly out from behind his tree, thudding on to the
earth below, and our job was done. I left Harry, still swearing volubly and rubbing his
shoulder, and crept back to the line of men I now knew so well.'

Above: *A Japanese sniper lies dead moments after being on the receiving end from a burst of machine-gun fire on the island of Saipan. The sniper had fired on a photographer, disclosing his hide.*

MOPPING-UP OPERATIONS

In his memoir of the war with Japan titled *Frankel-y Speaking About World War II In The South Pacific*, author Stanley Frankel recalled an effective method of dealing with snipers. As daylight waned, his unit did its best to secure a perimeter against nocturnal enemy prowlers on the island of New Georgia.

'The security platoon creeps and crawls to high ground,' Frankel wrote, 'fans out in a semicircle facing the enemy, and just watches. Danger is over, until dark. A tired sniper might risk a try at one of the sweaty, broad backs lying below him, but he's a punk shot. If he tries to fire more than once every hour, he is quickly spotted and cut into quarters with the "fixer", the Browning automatic rifle [BAR]. Two hundred yards [183m] behind the platoon, the company digs in furiously. Must be dug in, fed and bedded down by dark. Our jungle army shuts up shop at nightfall.'

Retired Air Force Technical Sergeant David W. Wittich relates the story of his father and a fellow 1st Division Marine dealing with snipers on Guadalcanal. 'There's quite a few mountains around Guadalcanal. One of these was home to a particularly nasty bunch of Japanese snipers, and they were shooting Marines daily – with impunity, because nobody could get up at them and get them out of the caves. Dad got together with a friend, Wade Brenneman, and the two of them gathered up all the satchel charges they could carry along with a length of rope – and headed for the mountain top. Once there, they tied the rope around a tree, lit the first charge and, like crazy Marines everywhere, took on the Japanese snipers! They jumped off the top of the mountain, swung across the face of the caves and threw the charges in.

'This worked for quite a few caves, until Dad missed one particular jump – apparently rather badly – and didn't make it back to the top on his swing. The charge was in the cave, along with the Japanese soldiers, and it went off just as Dad swung back across in front of the cave. Somehow, he managed to hang onto the rope but the swing changed direction – instead of swinging across the cave face, he now looped out over the valley, up and over the face of the mountain and landed in the tree that the rope was tied to – with something close to 50 bits of shrapnel from his

100

own charge buried within him. But, the mountain was now finally clear of snipers. They both got the Silver Star for what they did.'

By the end of World War II, the sniper had demonstrated his worth on the battlefield in every theatre of conflict. Although the nature of combat was continually changing, the adaptable and resourceful sniper was a proven asset.

THE BIG BOYS

During World War II, a number of weapons were employed in ways which probably had been unintended when they were introduced. While infantry usually opted to blast snipers out of their hides with heavy weapons such as the Browning 7.62mm (0.3in) and BAR (see picture), anti-tank guns, bazookas, artillery, and even air strikes were also employed against tenacious snipers who could not be easily rooted out. Another innovation during the war was the use of the heavy Browning M-2 0.50in (12.7mm) calibre machine gun in a sniper role. A single shot setting was available on the M-2, and when used by a skilled sniper the weapon proved deadly from an extreme distance. State-of-the-art 0.50in (12.7mm) calibre sniper arms such as the M82A1 Barrett 'Light Fifty' and the M107 trace their lineage to the experimentation with the M-2 more than half a century ago.

During the Korean War, instructors at a US Army sniper school discuss the operation of an M-2 carbine upgraded with a night scope. Originally introduced as the M-1 carbine in 1940, and widely used during World War II, more than six million examples across a number of variations were produced up until the 1960s. The weapon is little used today.

CHAPTER SIX

KOREA AND THE COLD WAR

Perhaps the most violent period in history, the half-century from 1950 to the new millennium spawned countless conflicts. From high stakes fighting on the Korean peninsula to proxy wars prosecuted around the globe, the sniper served his captain and his cause on a variety of fronts.

In the wake of World War II, the geopolitical situation across the globe was in the throes of unprecedented change. Contrasting ideological and economic visions of world order moved inevitably toward conflict.

From the devastation of the costliest war in history, the United States and the Soviet Union emerged as the two superpowers, and in Europe the democracies of the West and the Communist states of the East built up their defences in two armed camps. Eventually, these military and political alliances would be formalized by the founding of the North Atlantic Treaty Organization (NATO) and the Warsaw Pact. The Cold War, as the tense stand-off became known, lasted more than 40 years, with most historians acknowledging its conclusion with the tumbling down of the Berlin Wall.

Another significant phenomenon of the post-World War II era was the emergence of the Third World, those nations which were underdeveloped, in many instances heavily populated and often governed by unstable or totalitarian regimes. After the war, the era of colonialism faded rapidly, fuelling a wave of nationalism which swept Africa, Asia, the Americas and areas of historical unrest in Europe with renewed vigour.

Although East and West flirted with disaster on more than one occasion during the latter half of the twentieth century, direct fighting was averted. Instead, a series of proxy wars were waged. Each side probed for weaknesses in the other, whether in military or political resolve. The armed forces of the United States and Great Britain, sometimes with the support of a United Nations mandate, assumed the burden of containing Communism and maintaining stability during a period of considerable nation building and political tension which seemed to ebb and flow with regularity.

THE KOREAN WAR

In Europe, the flashpoint for open war would certainly be a divided Germany. Further adding to

Opposite: *Camouflaged to blend with the snowy landscape, two 1st Division US Marine scout-snipers aim a .30in (7.62mm) calibre rifle (foreground) and an M-1 sniper rifle at enemy positions.*

the concern was the divided city of Berlin, where troops of both sides stood virtually eyeball to eyeball. The Asian powderkeg was on the Korean peninsula. The Communist north and the democratic south had been divided along the 38th Parallel at the end of World War II. In June 1950, North Korean forces rolled into South Korea, initiating a bloody struggle that was halted three years later by a tenuous armistice. To this day, thousands of US and South Korean troops stare across the demilitarized zone (DMZ) at their Communist adversaries.

After World War II, the sniper was once again relegated to unimportance in the armed forces of the United States and Great Britain; however, with the outbreak of the Korean War, as casualties due to Communist sniper fire mounted, the pendulum swung quickly in the other direction. North Korean snipers, many of whom were Soviet trained, often utilized the familiar Moisin Nagant 1891/30 rifle equipped with telescopic sights. Later in the war, vast numbers of Chinese troops were deployed to assist North Korea, and with them came more capable snipers.

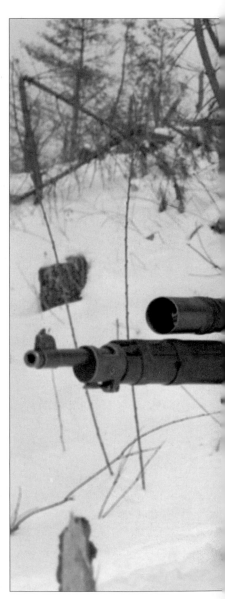

As the Korean War dragged on, it degenerated at times into a protracted stand-off, with each side staging raids against the other's fortified trench lines, as well as undertaking intermittent mortar and artillery barrages. Operations were limited by harsh, mountainous terrain and winter temperatures which regularly reached well below zero degrees Fahrenheit (minus 17.8 degrees Celsius). In *Stalk and Kill: The Sniper Experience*, Adrian Gilbert recounts a US Marine officer's illustration of the rapid change of heart among American soldiers as it related to snipers. The newly arrived commander of the 3rd Battalion, 1st Marine Regiment, attempted to survey enemy positions one morning.

'When the shell-scarred slopes became visible at first light, he placed his binoculars in the bunker opening and gazed out. Ping! A sniper bullet smashed the binoculars to the deck while blood welled up in the crease in his hand.

'The battalion commander, fortunately, was only scratched, but he reflected that it was a helluva situation when the CO could not even take a look at the ground he was defending without getting shot at. Right then and there he decided that something had to be done about the enemy sniper. Now was the time to bring in the pin-wheel boys – the Marines who could keep every shot within the V ring at five hundred yards.

'Sending for the S-4 [staff officer], the colonel learned that within the supply section there was an adequate number of rifles and telescopic sights. The colonel next sent for an experienced gunnery sergeant who had spent considerable time firing with rifle teams. He told the gunny what he wanted: he then sat back and waited. His expectations were completely fulfilled.'

'The gunny visited each company to pick sniper candidates. He outlined his requirements to the company commander. He wanted riflemen who possessed the characteristics of good infantrymen. But above all, he stressed the need for patience. This trait is absolutely essential, for a sniper must remain still and alert for long hours, waiting for the enemy to show himself.

'Each company sent a number of candidates, and the gunny selected approximately six two-man teams per company....

'Soon the range was ready, and the gunny began an intensive three-week course on sniping....

'Lying for hours with their rifles sighted up the draws, the sniper teams trained together daily, learning their new roles well. When they finished the gunny's sniper course, they were qualified snipers in every sense of the word, and their future performances readily proved it....

'At the time the snipers finished their special training, enemy artillery and mortars were daily peppering both the MLR [Main Line of Resistance] and the outposts. Enemy snipers seemed to be in control. Then the Marine sniper teams were sent out to the various outposts. To spur them on, a case of cold beer was awarded to the men of each outpost that got 12 kills within a week. All hands turned to in helping the rifle experts in spotting enemy snipers. The change in the situation was fantastic. "In nothing flat there was no more sniping on our positions", remembers the Bn CO.

'Only a week after the sniper teams went in to action, the division commander came to test their efficiency. Where only a week before men had hardly dared to stick up their heads, the two-star general strode the entire length of Item company's MLR, armed with nothing but his walking stick....'

COUNTER-SNIPER ACTION

The need for qualified snipers and counter-snipers was evident throughout the war on the Korean peninsula. 'Constant sniper fire was the scariest part of the war,'

Below: Seen with a trio of appropriate sniper scopes, this .30in (7.62mm) calibre sniper rifle was designed by a US Army officer and employed during the Korean War.

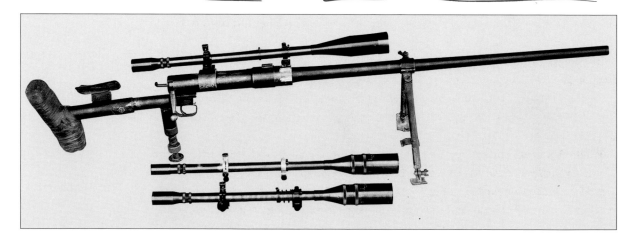

SPRINGFIELD 1903A4

Country of Origin	United States
Calibre	0.30in (7.62mm)
Overall length	1097mm (43.2in)
Barrel length	610mm (24in)
Weight	3.94kg (8.7lb)

Bernie Resnick, a veteran of a combat engineer battalion, told the *Eagle-Tribune*, a New England regional newspaper. 'Snipers were in the hills; they were everywhere,' he said. 'And there were North Korean soldiers in civilian uniforms. On my first job of driving a grader, the sniper bullets were so close you could hear what sounded like the snapping of a whip at a circus. It was the sweetest sound in the world when you would hear that because you knew the bullet had missed you.'

One of the most heroic chapters in US military history was the defence of and withdrawal from the frozen confines of the Chosin Reservoir in the autumn of 1950. General S.L.A. Marshall, a well-known historian, called the combat some of the most violent small-unit fighting in the history of American warfare. He praised the combined efforts of the 1st Marine Division, as well as attached US Army units and a contingent of British Royal Marines.

A member of the Army's 7th Division, James Collins, told reporter Eugene Sutherland of his unit's rearguard assignment. 'That's when my buddy got killed,' he remembered. 'We were bringing up the rear. There was a road that cut into the mountains. He darted across and hit the ditch. I darted right behind him. A sniper got him. He was lying dead in the ditch. I was left by myself.'

In *Sniper*, author Adrian Gilbert adds that Marine Sergeant Bill Krilling was dramatically affected by events in Korea. 'One day after a close friend was killed by a communist sniper, while moving about the area, the man sent to recover my dead friend was also killed by the same sniper. I decided there and then to become a sniper.'

While American snipers commonly used the Springfield Model 1903 rifle or the C and D variants of the M-1 Garand, British and Australian snipers were most often armed with the Enfield No. 4 Mk I or the vintage P14/No. 3 Mk I. Innovation can produce remarkable results, and the telescopic-sighted Browning M-2 heavy machine gun set to fire a single shot could indeed increase the range for a sniper up to 1100m

(1200 yards). At times, distance dictated that a sniper work in tandem with an automatic weapon such as the Browning Automatic Rifle (BAR) or a machine gun.

SEEING THE 'FUZZ'

Gunnery Sergeant Francis H. Killeen, Gilbert notes, received his first live sniping experience at Su Dong Ni. 'We got into a ditch alongside the road, and I immediately figured our range would be [365m] 400 yards uphill. I looked through my 8-power scope and could spot an otherwise unseen line of riflemen firing down at us by seeing the "fuzz" of their projectiles. Lieutenant Davis, our 60mm [2.3in] mortar man, was right beside me. I told him where the enemy fire was coming from and in less than a minute he had three mortars in action and the fire lifted. We attacked and took the positions.

'This was the first time I found my sniper gun to be more effective than my M1 rifle. Usually we were in close actions where the M1's rapid fire could be more important than the long-range capability, but this time we were looking over a big valley at ridges [457 to 545m] 500 to 600 yards across the way. I chose a rock on the far ridge and got my lieutenant to spot my strikes with his binoculars. In that way, I made sure my rifle was still shooting where I aimed.

Below: *During a dangerous sniper clearance mission against North Korean troops, members of an American patrol crouch as a comrade prepares to return fire.*

'In the late afternoon, columns of enemy began moving into position for evening festivities. I got off a couple of rounds, but without a spotter I could not tell if I was making hits. I got a BAR man to register his rifle on the same rock I had used for zeroing. When he had his sights right we tried some team shooting.

'When I located the enemy I fired tracer at him or them. Although tracer is lighter than the AP we were using, the trajectory was close enough and the BAR man, who could not see the enemy soldiers with his iron sights, simply attempted to catch my tracer with his bullets. The idea was to hammer the enemy with a decent volume of fire in the hopes that if I missed, the BAR man would get him.

'The technique was instantly popular, and I soon had a big light machine-gun and two more BARs creating the biggest beaten zone I ever saw. My lieutenant ... got more riflemen into the fray, and we had the enemy falling all along their wood line.'

HIT AND RUN

Following his first sniper action at Su Dong Ni, Gunnery Sergeant Francis H. Killeen recalled the uncomfortable end to the action:

'In the heat of the action, and with the obvious success we were enjoying, I forgot about the "hit and run" rule. We have to remember that the other guys also have people who can shoot. A bullet about one click low reminded me, and I cleared out just as a few more came into where I had just been.'

HEAVY FIRE

In addition to conventional counter-sniping efforts, soldiers of both sides regularly employed greater firepower to dislodge or silence enemy snipers. To commemorate the fiftieth anniversary of the Korean War, the US Department of Defense undertook an initiative to record the wartime memories of Korean War veterans. A member of a US Air Force forward air control unit, Harold K. Gower, recalled an effective method of dealing with a North Korean sniper's nocturnal fire.

'There was a graves registration unit across the road from our checkpoint and we visited with them frequently,' Gower recalled. 'Also, we had a persistent sniper who would wait until a vehicle approached the checkpoint after dark and then fire one or two shots at our location. We were never hit, but the ricochet was scary. To end his harassment, we drove a jeep that had a [12.7mm] .50-calibre machine gun mounted in the back down to our position after dark. We had arranged for the ammunition belt to be loaded with extra incendiary shells and we waited for our sniper. When he fired, the machine gunner aimed at the sniper flash and fired a prolonged burst. It appeared to be a steady stream of fire going up the opposite hill. We never attempted to climb the hill and see if our sniper had been hit, but we never had any more firing at our location.'

One retired warrant officer wrote to the Department of Defense that he had been only a child during the Korean War. Years later, after joining the army, he listened to his platoon sergeant tell the story of a company commander who went to the front line each day when the Chinese dinnertime routine was being followed. The story

RISKY BUSINESS

John E. Boitnott, a platoon sergeant with the 3rd Battalion, 5th Marine Regiment, chanced upon a tactic that amounted to risky business for his buddy, which proved successful nonetheless. According to author Gilbert, Boitnott was working with Pfc Henry Friday, who was acting as his spotter and apparently was not overly apprehensive about the hazardous duty.

'Our position was outpost Yorke, about [3.2km] two miles forward of our front line and due north of the place where the peace talks were taking place,' Boitnott related. 'We were on the northern parapet of our hill, watching the valley for hostile movement. Friday suggested it was his turn for breakfast and asked permission to go through the centre trench to the reverse slope for chow. The centre trench ran sort of perpendicular to the front and had to be rushed through before an enemy took a crack at you.

'I was lying along the forward parapet and when Friday ran through someone took a shot at him. I thought I saw movement on a hill mass across the valley. The area was about [613m] 670 yards away. I called to Friday and told him to come to me. As Friday cleared the trench the enemy sniper rose again to fire, and this time I saw him clearly. One shot, one dead North Korean sniper. Lt. Johnson verified the kill and reported it to the company commander.

'Friday and I teamed up, with him running the trench and me shooting the enemy for two more kills, which seemed to entertain about everybody on our side. Shortly thereafter word of our "operation" reached someone less imaginative and we had to knock it off. Over a two-day span, I made nine confirmed kills in nine shots from [612 to 1143m] 670 to 1250 yards.'

goes that a soldier would carry a bucket of rice down the same path at the same time every day. Setting a 0.50in (12.7mm) calibre machine gun to single fire, the company commander would shoot the replacement delivery boy, turn around, and return to his headquarters.

In *One Shot–One Kill*, Charles W. Sasser and Craig Roberts recorded the encounter on 21 May 1952 between an American patrol from the 5th Marine Regiment, commanded by Lieutenant Gil Holmes, and a Chinese unit attempting to penetrate their lines.

'A rifle squad travelled on each flank to cover the sniper teams as the patrol slipped into the pulverized terrain lighted by a weak spring sun. Taking advantage of cover … [t]he Marines crept cautiously to within [366m] 400 yards of the entrenched enemy on Hill 719.

'The scout sniper patrol left its two reinforcing squads at a vantage point on high ground about [247m] 300 yards outside Dog Company's lines because we felt such a large force would preclude our hopes for a surprise attack,' recalled the lieutenant. 'Throughout the course of our approach to hill 719, our objective was always in plain sight and a certain amount of enemy activity could be observed on the skyline as we made our way forward.

'Naturally we took full advantage of the defilade and concealment available, but I will never cease to wonder how we got so close to the main battle positions without detection. After we were ordered to break contact and withdraw I do recall that we were momentarily caught in an automatic cross-fire from both flanks and, if I am any judge of such matters, it did not come from the Chinese MLR [Main Line of Resistance] so it is barely possible that we did penetrate a very thin screening force without knowing it.

'We finally reached a ridge top roughly parallel to the entrenchments on 719 from which we could look across and see a couple of Chinese wandering around the area in an unconcerned manner. I would say that the range from our position was about [366m] 400 yards …

'We were all spread along the ridge in a loose skirmish line with sights adjusted, waiting for remunerative targets. I finally spotted three at the same time and gave the word to cut loose. That really did it!

Below: *A telltale hole in the helmet of a sprawled UN soldier discloses the cause of death on a desolate Korean plain. In Korea, both sides used snipers with deadly effect.*

'I had no idea what a hornet's nest they had over there. They came running out of their bunkers along the trench to their battle stations, but it soon was obvious they were rather fouled up.

'They tried to set up a machine gun to our direct front and one of my boys knocked off the gunner. When they finally got the gun in action they opened up on an area at least [183m] 200 yards from our left flank. Some joker, evidently the company commander, was running around like a madman trying to square things away, but his people were crumbling up all around him under a steady stream of the well-aimed fire of our sharpshooters.

'Soon after we opened fire, Dog Company called us back in. I stuck my neck out and held the position for another fifteen minutes after receiving the order because we had good shooting and the Chinese just couldn't seem to get squared away …

'As we pulled out we received automatic weapon cross-fire from our flanks, but it was well overhead. I figured there was a fair chance we'd be intercepted on the way in, so we withdrew by bounds – half covering the other half.

'Approximately three-quarters of an hour after we broke contact and commenced our withdrawal from 719 we were safely back inside our own lines without spilling a drop of Marine blood – it was a good day!'

Below: *Their helmets festooned with pine branches, a US sniper team is tested during training, 1952. The sniper aims an M-1 Garand rifle fitted with an M 82 telescopic sight.*

SNIPER RIFLES IN KOREA

With the outbreak of hostilities on the Korean peninsula in 1950, the upper hand in sniping was initially with the Communist forces. They employed a variety of rifles, including weapons which had been supplied by the United States to the armies of Nationalist China during World War II and the reliable Soviet-made Moisin Nagant Model 1891/30.

United Nations forces fielded virtually no trained snipers early in the Korean War, and when they did begin training in earnest it was in response to Communist successes. US snipers used the M-1C, M-1D and the venerable Springfield 1903, while Commonwealth sharpshooters were often equipped with the World War I era P14/No. 3 Mk I (T) or the Enfield No. 4 Mk I (T). The US armed forces were not equipped with the updated M-14 rifle until 1957, four years after the armistice was signed at Panmunjom.

FORWARD POSITIONS

Snipers continued to perform in their intelligence-gathering role during the Korean War, many times identifying targets and calling heavier firepower into the engagement. As a platoon commander with the 3rd Royal Australian Regiment, Lieutenant Allan Limburg coordinated such an effort against the enemy which he referred to as 'Charlie', a term which would become more familiar over a decade later in Vietnam.

'Two battalion snipers were allocated to my platoon,' Limburg remembered. 'They kept the enemy's heads down during the day. One day, while firing at them, they were amused to see Charlie waving a shovel from side to side, signalling a "washout", "you've missed me". A prime aim of both sides in defence is to stop the enemy getting supplies to their forward troops. Charlie could not replenish his forward positions during the day as we overlooked them. He did this at night. Instead of using the difficult route forward, in his trenches, he preferred to take the easy way, above ground. From under our camouflage-netted fire pit, using binoculars, our snipers and I often observed heavily laden parties of twenty or more Chinese moving forward just on dusk.

'"Why not have a go at the buggers, Skip?" they asked. To be successful all fire would have to land simultaneously before they dived into their trenches. I planned a codeword to call all our fire down. When used over the radio the Kiwi guns opened up first. It took about 24 seconds for their shells to land. When the Centurion tank crew heard the artillery shells overhead, they commenced firing. Their shot took about six seconds. When we heard the shells my two [12.7mm] .50 calibre machine guns opened up. We used it several times to great effect.'

PITCHED BATTLE

Pulitzer Prize winning reporter Fred Sparks was with the US 187th Parachute Regiment near the Korean town of Inje. He watched the paratroopers fight a pitched battle with Chinese troops who had little regard for their own lives.

'Chinese got on the hills on both sides of the narrow road and zeroed-in machine guns and artillery,' Sparks wrote for the *Chicago Daily News* edition of 4 June 1951. 'In one instance a fanatical Chinese stood on a cliff and simply dropped a grenade down on a jeep. I saw mortars bursting on the road behind my vehicle. Scores of vehicles were knocked out. Chinese snipers wearing green uniforms and using no-flash rifles peppered us at will. They couldn't be seen in the thick growth. One jeep driver ahead of me quietly slumped over his wheel, a sneak bullet in his right ear. Several "Suitcase Charlies" – fanatical Chinese carrying valise-shaped explosives – ran up to a few tanks and tossed their packages between the treads. But like a covered wagon train in the wild west Indian days we pulled our way through the comparatively primitive foe ... I can now author a book entitled, "I was a Duck in a Shooting Gallery."'

North Korean and Chinese Communist troops proved to be tough, resourceful and ruthless foes. Sasser and Roberts tell the story of US Army Corporal Chet Hamilton near the famous Pork Chop Hill as he was sent forward to assist attacking GIs who were being roughly handled during an assault which ultimately failed.

'The GIs who made it to the hill started up the slope,' recalled Hamilton. 'The grade was so steep they tugged at rocks and bushes to assist them. The more heavily burdened with machine guns and flamethrowers straggled, while skirmishers broke into little pockets to continue the assault.

'I felt helpless watching from the sandbagged trenches ... until I noticed something. It was only about [366m] 400 yards across the valley from the Chinese lines. My position put me on almost the same level with the chink defenders on the other hill. In order for the Chicoms to see our troops and fire at them down through their wire as the GIs charged up the hill, they had to lean up and out over their trenches, exposing wide patches of their quilted hides.

'That was all I needed.

'It had become clear morning in spite of the smoke and dust boiling above the Chinese hill. The four-power magnification of my scope made the chinks leap right into my face. All I had to do was go down the trench line, settle the post-and-horizontal-line reticle on one target right after the other, and squeeze the trigger. It

HOT SHOT

US Army Corporal Chet Hamilton recalled the havoc he wrought among Chinese trenches when assisting an attack:

'The GIs never made it past the chink wire ... By the time the GIs withdrew from the hill, dashing from rock to rock, demoralized and defeated, my gun barrel was so hot to the touch that I could hardly touch it ... I know I shot at least forty chinks before the attack bogged down and the enemy went back to their burrows. Bodies had to be stacked up in the Chinese trenches.'

was a lot like going to a carnival and shooting those little toy crows off the fence. *Bap!* The crow disappeared and you moved over to the next crow. By the time you got to the end of the fence, you came back to the beginning and the crows were all lined up again ready for you to start over. I don't know who the Chinese first sergeant was over there, but he kept throwing up another crow for me every minute or two. And I kept knocking them off the fence. The fight for the hill lasted about two hours. The other guys ... came to watch, point out targets, and cheer when I zapped one.'

PALESTINE

In the years following World War II, troops of the British Commonwealth were called upon many times to maintain order and stability in regions where their colonial rule had once dominated. A Communist insurgency in Malaya conducted a campaign of armed terror from 1948 until the country was declared safe enough in 1957 to become an independent member of the Commonwealth.

During the first six months of 1948, British forces were withdrawing from Palestine, and 40 Commando of the Royal Marines was charged with maintaining order between the Jewish and Arab citizenry in the port city of Haifa on the eve of the birth of the nation of Israel. 'As it happened, the evacuation was completed without incident but when it was decided that 40 Commando would be the last British unit to leave Palestine, the situation was tense and a peaceful withdrawal seemed very uncertain,' reported the unit's intelligence section.

Below: From the safety of his dugout, a US soldier scans enemy lines for a likely target through the scope of his M-1 Garand rifle.

One morning, a British armoured vehicle came under attack, and the commando unit was forced to engage in urban counter-sniper warfare. 'Shortly before 1000 hrs,' the intelligence section said, 'the Jews opened fire on the Arab village outside No. 1 Gate, and battles commenced in various areas. An hour later one of our Staghounds [armoured cars] became involved in an exchange of fire in Bank Street. Two British policemen had been shot and the Staghound gave covering fire while they were being evacuated. The sniper was located and three direct hits with 37mm [1.45in] shells from the Staghound silenced him forever.'

Later, other hotspots erupted, and the commandos confronted multiple snipers, some of whom were actually using automatic weapons. 'In the afternoon a Jewish Bren gun sniper was causing considerable confusion firing at traffic along Kingsway. His position behind an armoured plated window was impervious to Bren fire, which was returned from one of our positions,' noted the intelligence section. 'Three PIAT bombs, however, effectively silenced the offending sniper. A little later a Jewish Bren gunner wounded Lt. A.H.W. Seed, RM, in the back of the head with a deliberate burst of fire at one of our forward positions. Lt. Seed was evacuated to the British Military Hospital. A patrol of one corporal and two Marines immediately went out, located the sniper, and eliminated him. At approximately the same time, our position on the British Sailors' Society's club by No. 3 Gate silenced three snipers firing on the Gate.'

ADEN

The southern portion of the Arabian peninsula, particularly in the vicinity of the city of Aden, was the scene of four years of unrest during the mid-1960s. Various Arab factions fought one another, as well as British troops, for control of the area. On 30 April 1964, Royal Marine 45 Commando moved to secure high ground in an area called the Dhanaba Basin. In a coordinated assault, B Company, 3rd Battalion, the Parachute Regiment, was to leave its base in Aden and jump into the Wadi Taym and hold a hill called Cap Badge. The operation was ultimately successful but costly to the paras, who were in peril for 30 hours and fought a 10-hour gunbattle.

'The Company Commander, Major Peter Walter, led the leading platoon to clear one fort while the rest of the Company assaulted the village, driving out the dissidents and killing several in the process,' authors James Paul and Martin Spirit wrote. 'A determined group of the enemy managed to move in behind the leading troops and started a surprise attack. They were themselves then ambushed by the rear element of the Company under the Second-in-Command, Captain Barry Jewkes and all of the enemy party were killed. Enemy snipers from the slopes above the village now opened … fire causing several casualties. These snipers were in dead ground to the Marines above who were unable to help and ground attack Hunters [aircraft] were called in to help. Despite this, casualties continued to mount. Captain Jewkes was killed, another soldier was killed and six more wounded.'

Opposite: Armed with an early version of the Self-Loading Rifle (SLR), a British sniper (right) and his spotter from the 3rd Battalion, the Parachute Regiment, scan the mountain crags along a potential enemy supply route during the Radfan crisis, Aden, 1957.

According to Adrian Gilbert in *Sniper*, the most bitter fighting in Aden itself took place at an area called Crater where British troops had been ambushed. A battalion of the Argyll and Sutherland Highlanders supported by 45 Commando was assigned to clear Crater, which actually was a system of streets and alleys built inside the crater of an extinct volcano.

The Commando snipers 'painstakingly clambered up the precipitous crags which surrounded Crater,' wrote Gilbert. 'There they were able to take up positions overlooking the city, and look for enemy activity. For a period of ten days the Commando snipers fired down into the crater.' A pair of snipers from 45 Commando dispatched 11 Arab terrorists and wounded five others while firing 25 rounds of ammunition.

Gilbert tells the story of one British sniper at Crater. 'The Argylls under Mad Mitch [Lieutenant Colonel Colin Mitchell, CO of the Argyll and Sutherland Highlanders] made all the news when they retook Crater, but without us they'd never have done it without taking lots of casualties. It was us who wore the Arabs down, and made them realize that they couldn't have it all their own way. We were right up above the town and I could look through my telescopic sight and see them moving about. We waited for hours. The heat was incredible, bouncing off the rocks and burning you to a turn. But it was worth it, when I saw an Arab coming out of

Below: Royal Marine Lance Corporal John Tilley secures his sniper position at the bitterly contested Crater, near embattled Aden, June 1967.

RIFLE L42A1

Country of Origin	Great Britain
Calibre	7.62mm (0.30in)
Overall length	1181mm (46.5in)
Barrel length	699mm (27.5in)
Weight	4.43kg (9.76lb)

a mosque carrying a rifle. I knew he was a terrorist; we'd found out that they used mosques as meeting places. As he walked up this alleyway towards me I took aim. He couldn't see me, of course. And then I squeezed the trigger, and he fell backwards, dropping his rifle. I'd definitely got him. Everyone else around him ran off in panic, leaving him lying there until nightfall.'

Another successful Royal Marine sniper at Aden was Mick Harrison, a one-time poacher, who killed or wounded eight Arab terrorists with 18 rounds during a four-day foray. In an interview with Gilbert, Harrison talked of his tactics.

'The terrorists in Aden had been shooting up the Argylls or the Northumberland Fusiliers and they wanted snipers, so I was called for. I got in the back of a Land Rover, and they had got my kit, my rifle and scope. I checked my ammunition – Vickers [7.62mm] .303 7Z rounds. They told me to go up the mountain, and for fourteen hours a day, for four days, I made my base in an old, ruined Turkish fort. Each morning I hauled myself up with a rope while it was still dark, around 5.30 or 6.00. When I got up there I hid. The important thing wasn't to go popping off at anything. I saw I was all right for water before I went up, and in that climate you needed plenty. It was just a question of using training. Just a matter, so to speak, of giving the other man enough rope to hang himself.

'I had to make the terrorists show themselves. What I did was to expose myself to them deliberately. I'd kill one, then I'd move to a new position. They were about [366 to 457m] 400 to 500 yards away. I'd get up and wave to them to draw their attention. It was the old idea of bringing your quarry to you. They thought they were good and I let them come to me. The first person I shot came out all dressed in black, and I remember I shot him in the throat. They wanted to go to Allah's garden, and I just paved the way for them.'

As late as the 1960s, many British snipers were still using the No. 4 Mk I rifle, while the standard issue infantry weapon became the L1A1. Snipers were

Above: *Israeli paratroopers respond after coming under fire from PLO snipers on the Israel–Lebanon border. Israeli forces have long experience of dealing with snipers in urban environments.*

disappointed with the performance of the L1A1, and a heavier version of the No. 4 Mk I was issued to them. This weapon, designated the L42A1, was equipped with a heavier barrel which could accept the NATO 7.62mm (0.30in) cartridge. Canadian and Australian snipers were fielded with the Parker Hale 1200 TX, which had been built for sniping. In the late 1950s, the US Army improved the M-1 design with a 7.62mm (0.30in) cartridge compatible rifle called the M-14.

ISRAEL

While the British armed forces were engaged on the Arabian peninsula, a coalition of Arab states was at war with Israel. In what turned out to be a resounding victory for Israel during the Six-Day War of 1967, the Israel Defense Forces (IDF) made territorial gains with the capture of the Golan Heights and Gaza. The Israelis were also victorious against Jordanian troops in the holy city of Jerusalem.

A fortified position known as Ammunition Hill was contested by Jordanian legionnaires of the al-Hussein Battalion and a company of paratroopers from Battalion 66 of the IDF. In one fortified position on Ammunition Hill, called

Antenna House, Jordanian snipers and machine gunners occupied the upper floors, firing from the windows. As the Israelis cleared trenches of enemy troops, they became exposed and were targeted by the snipers. At an even higher elevation, the IDF soldiers were sniped at by Jordanians ensconced at Givat HaMivtar.

The Israelis were required to silence a network of reinforced bunkers, using explosive charges and calling in tank support. The foremost of these positions actually contained a smaller bunker within a larger outer concrete structure with walls 40cm (16in) thick. Grenades and bazooka fire produced no telling results, and eventually the bunker was cracked open by a blast of 16kg (35lb) of TNT. Tanks were finally able to silence the snipers atop Givat HaMivtar. In one of the sharpest engagements of the short war, the IDF suffered 24 killed and 90 wounded. Only 20 paratroopers were unhurt. Seventy-one Jordanians died.

Simultaneously, another company of Battalion 66 engaged Arab resistance in a neighbourhood called Sheikh Jarra. Enemy snipers fired from numerous rooftops, impeding the IDF progress toward the first of its objectives, St John's Hospital. The arduous advance continued street by street and house by house as the sniper positions were silenced one at a time.

The wars, police actions and peacekeeping events of the latter half of the twentieth century reinforced the necessity for armies to comprehend the ability of the sniper to influence tactics on the battlefield. However, post-war expediency resulted in the tightening of defence budgets in numerous nations, and sniper training waned even during such a period of unrest. Even after their Korean experience, only when significant numbers of troops were deployed to Vietnam did US commanders feel, once again, the sense of urgency to deploy effective snipers.

FORTUNES OF WAR

During the Yom Kippur War of 1973, an Israeli paratrooper was preparing to drop into Jerusalem. Rabbi Mordechai Katz recounted his potentially lifesaving decision.

'Snipers were shooting at the soldiers as they descended, so the paratroopers had to travel very lightly. The paratrooper assembled his backpack with great care. He then came upon his Tefillin [Jewish laws contained in two small black boxes]; he was about to leave them behind on the plane, when he reconsidered. "These Tefillin have been with me wherever I've gone", he thought to himself. "Perhaps having the words of Hashem with me when I jump will bring me good fortune." Consequently, he put the bag into the backpack as well and jumped. The snipers' fire was there to greet him when he landed. He managed to scurry to safety and later examined himself and his belongings. The first thing he removed was his Tefillin. Immediately, he noticed a bullet hole in his Tefillin and the bullet lodged in the siddur which had been in his Tefillin bag! "It's a good thing I decided to take my Tefillin along", said the soldier. "If I hadn't, that bullet would have gone through my bag and into my body".'

A US Marine instructor prompts a sniper student, who peers through the scope of his Remington Model 700 rifle. Many snipers were actually trained in Vietnam itself during the war. A robust weapon suited to the rigours of jungle combat, the Remington 700 was a development of the USMC M40 sniper rifle.

CHAPTER SEVEN

THE VIETNAM WAR

Stalking the jungles, hills and rice paddies of Indochina, the sniper gained almost mythical stature during the Vietnam War (1961–73). Tales of his stealth still astonish the public, perpetuate his legend and ensure that his skill remains prized.

From the end of European colonialism through the era of the containment policy and into a lengthy period of national introspection for the United States, the Vietnam War ebbed and flowed in Southeast Asia for nearly three decades. With the bitter defeat of the French by the Communist Viet Minh at Dien Bien Phu in 1954, the future of a pro-Western government in the southern portion of the divided Vietnam appeared to be in serious jeopardy. In subsequent years, the United States embarked on a programme of growing military involvement in a struggle pitting ideological and nationalistic fervour against the perception of a clear threat to democracy in the form of advancing Communist-backed militarism on the Asian continent.

North Vietnam, a surrogate of the Communist superpowers, actively supported a ruthless grassroots guerrilla movement collectively known as the Viet Minh and later the Viet Cong. Inspired by Ho Chi Minh, their leader during most of the conflict, the Viet Cong conducted a campaign of terror across the Vietnamese countryside. They targeted civilians. Employing effective hit-and-run tactics, they often ambushed US and South Vietnamese patrols, then vanished into the jungle. They infiltrated enemy bases, firing rockets and automatic weapons at seemingly safe positions. At the same time, the well-organized and well-led North Vietnamese Army conducted operations in strength in the south.

The troops of the US Army and Marine Corps experienced some of the most difficult fighting in their histories as they coped with inhospitable terrain, climatic extremes and a determined, resourceful foe. Major engagements were relatively few during the American military involvement in Vietnam. In virtually every case in which a pitched battle was fought, US and South Vietnamese forces could be considered the victors. However, bringing large numbers of the enemy to combat and winning a decisive victory proved virtually impossible against the Viet Cong, whose tactics were unconventional

Above: *Halted near a clearing by an enemy sniper outside Nha Trang, US soldiers attempt to dislodge their adversary with direct small-arms fire and grenades.*

and whose willingness to absorb horrific casualties and continue a lengthy war of attrition did not flag.

In contrast, more than 58,000 Americans died in Vietnam. A fiery debate over the morality of American involvement in the conflict, its apparent lack of progress toward a successful conclusion and its financial cost eventually pressed the US government to implement an exit strategy. The escalation of the war destroyed the presidency of Lyndon Johnson, who chose not to run for re-election in 1968. Richard Nixon was swept to power that year, and a programme of Vietnamization began to reduce the number of US combat troops in the country, which had peaked at more than a half million.

During Nixon's second term, the United States completed its withdrawal from Vietnam. Nixon, however, was forced from office by the Watergate scandal and replaced by Gerald Ford. In April 1975, Communist tanks rolled through the streets of the former South Vietnamese capital city, Saigon. Images of the evacuation of American diplomats and thousands of South Vietnamese refugees were burned into the American psyche. Indeed, the psychological wounds of the Vietnam War are still healing more than 30 years later. The Vietnam War was not lost in the rice paddies and jungles of Southeast Asia, but on the streets of American cities.

VIETNAMESE SNIPERS

Through much of American military history, the perceived worth of the sniper waxed and waned in the higher echelons of the US military command. So it was with Vietnam. Only a few Marine Corps and Army officers remained committed to a sniper doctrine. The North Vietnamese Army, on the other hand, incorporated the sniper into dedicated units of company strength.

Although it was relatively common to refer to the source of enemy fire as a 'sniper', a well-defined programme of sniper development existed among the Communists. North Vietnamese snipers were all volunteers who underwent a two-month training regimen before moving southward along the supply route known as the Ho Chi Minh Trail. These soldiers cooperated with their Viet Cong comrades and passed along rudimentary sniper training to the guerrillas.

The most prevalent sniper rifle used by the Communists was the World War II vintage Moisin Nagant Model 1891/30 equipped with telescopic sights. Relatively aged but still effective, the weapon was used in harassing fire against fixed positions or from ambush against the front, flanks and even the rear of an enemy patrol.

As in previous conflicts, a well-trained and motivated sniper was capable of holding large bodies of troops at bay. In *Sniper*, author Adrian Gilbert relates this type of occurrence.

'One such instance was observed by a Marine sniper, Joseph T. Ward, who described how a communist sniper had pinned down a neighbouring company of Marines. Although an air strike had been called, low cloud prevented the three-strong flight of F-4 Phantoms from attacking for over two hours. During this time, whenever a Marine moved he was picked off by the sniper. Even after the first strike of napalm, the sniper continued his work, wounding another man before departing the scene as the second strike went in. Obliged to admire the skill of the persistent sniper, Ward recalled: "While we cleaned our rifles, I thought what a day's worth one of Uncle Ho's best had given. One enemy sniper had killed three grunts, wounded four, tied up two companies and six fighter-bombers a good part of the day, and we hadn't seen any sign of him."'

The challenges of jungle and mountainous terrain along with the need for rapid mobility and firepower brought the helicopter to the forefront of American operations in Vietnam. North Vietnamese snipers were instructed to fire on the helicopters as they hovered above landing zones (LZ), disgorged troops or acted as spotters for units on the ground. Once their adversaries were in the field, the snipers logically targeted officers, operators of heavier weapons such as mortars and machine guns, and radiomen, in order to disrupt command and control, fire and manoeuvre and communications.

Below: US Army Specialist 4 John Rice uses the scope of his M-14 sniper rifle to scan a section of the Vietnamese countryside in this photo taken in 1970.

In August 1965, a company of Marines was met with heavy sniper fire as it attempted to come in on a dangerous landing zone (LZ). Archivist Ed Nicholls of the Operation Starlite Survivors Association transcribed the incident from official reports.

'Co. H 2/4 set down on LZ Blue and formed a hasty defence. The surroundings were a hodgepodge of rice paddies, streams, hedgerows and small wooded thickets approximately one kilometer [1093 yards] square in size bordered by the villages of An Thuong 2 on the north, Nam Yen 3 on the south and An Cuong 2 to the east. At first everything appeared normal in the tranquil atmosphere, but as the second wave of choppers dropped off the Marines, the sharp crack of Viet Cong snipers filled the air.

'LCpl Jimmy Brooks, a tall, amiable Southerner they called "The Buzzard" tumbled off the noisy "bird". Thinking he had tripped, a Marine rushed to his aid. As the individual cradled him in his arms, he noticed a gaping hole where the bullet had exited his back. Brooks died later. There was a scurry for cover as the volume of fire grew in intensity. A door gunner had his jaw ripped off. One sergeant caught a round in the throat. Capt. Howard B. Henry, a pilot from HMM-361, later recalled: "You just have to close your eyes and drop down to the deck."'

NARROW ESCAPE

On a mission to resupply an outlying jungle position, infantryman Michael Belis recalls an encounter with a sniper while unloading supplies:

'As we were filling canteens, a sniper in the opposite tree line fired a shot that literally went right between me and Utah [a fellow soldier]. We dove into the pile of limbs just as his second shot cracked overhead. His third shot smacked into the limbs and made us burrow deeper into the tangle of branches, nearer to the ground ...'

North Vietnamese and Viet Cong snipers often succeeded in demoralizing and harassing US troops. At times, mundane activities could be disrupted by a bullet fired from a hidden position, the finger of an unseen enemy on the trigger. Company C, 1st Battalion, 22nd Infantry Regiment, occupied a jungle position between An Khe and Kontum for four months in 1970. Supplies of every description had to be carried in from helicopter landing zones. Michael Belis wrote of a sniper encounter during one such resupply effort.

'About 20 minutes to half an hour later we heard brush breaking in the jungle at our end of the LZ, halfway to the sniper's tree line ... then a whole lot of shouted curses. It was the unmistakable voice of Livingston, our squad leader for the first squad ... Livingston had led the rest of the squad around the LZ to go get the sniper, but had run into growth so thick they couldn't get through it ...

'After things quieted down the sniper popped off another round, just to let us know he was still there. Half an hour or so after that, the guys yelled out to us to get ready to run toward our side of the LZ. They were calling in artillery on the opposite tree line, and would lay down cover fire with M-60s for us ... Not but a few seconds later the artillery began impacting on the far side of the LZ. Sometime after it finished ... a patrol ... found neither hide nor hair of the sniper.'

UNDER FIRE ✓

Australian troops, along with small contingents from other countries, also fought the Communists in Vietnam. The 5th Battalion, Royal Australian Regiment, engaged the Viet Cong during a nine-day stretch from 17 to 26 October 1966.

Captain Robert O'Neill of the regimental association wrote, 'But as they were about to climb out through the rocks on the far side, a shot rang out and Corporal Womal fell, yelling that he had been hit. A bullet had passed through his neck ...'

A Sioux helicopter was called to the scene to evacuate wounded Diggers, including Womal. 'Captain Bob Supple guided the aircraft in,' O'Neill continued. 'An additional danger that the pilot had to face was the risk of being shot down by an enemy sniper from the group further up the slope ... the snipers knew where Womal lay and could shoot anyone moving to his assistance. Although the Anti-Tank Platoon could neutralize the Viet Cong by covering fire for a short time it was doubtful if they could keep the fire up long enough to extract Womal.

'Despite ... orders to the contrary, the Platoon stretcher bearer, Private Fraser, began to crawl forward to Womal, under fire. He reached Womal and proceeded to dress his wound, placing his own body between Womal and the enemy in order to shield Womal from further fire. The snipers opened up again, missing Fraser by inches. In the meantime, the stretcher party which Lieutenant Deak had organized was moving forward under the direction of Sergeant Calvert and protected by the covering fire of the remainder of the platoon. By this time, the enemy had learned to recognize the voice of Deak as that of the leader. Each time he shouted orders bullets flew overhead from the snipers … However, the extraction was successful and the stretcher party struggled back to the cover of the rocks …'

THE US RESPONSE

As American operations in Vietnam expanded, the number of casualties grew, and most of these were the result of mines, booby traps and sniper fire. In order to counter the enemy sniper threat, the Marines took the lead in sniper training in Vietnam. Army sniper development lagged behind as doctrine actually restricted their use to operations within unit structures as opposed to Marine deployment of snipers into forward positions, often not only in the company of a spotter but also supported by a fire team or squad for defensive purposes. While Marine snipers were selected on the basis of numerous criteria, Army snipers were often simply the 'best shots' in the company.

Captain Robert A. Russell and Captain Jim Land had been the keepers of the 'sniper's flame' within the US Marine Corps. In the spring of 1965, Russell established the first Marine sniper school in Vietnam, training members of the 3rd Division. Land had operated a sniper school in Hawaii as early as 1960, and several months later he was charged with establishing a sniper school for 1st Division Marines. Both officers tested their tactics in the field as they developed their sniper programmes. Eventually, the sniper training programmes 'in country' were to last

Below: During the 1968 Tet Offensive, a pair of Viet Cong insurgents armed with Soviet-made World War II era SKS rifles take cover in the midst of an attack against South Vietnamese positions.

TO SEE IN THE DARK

To a limited degree, American and German forces both used primitive night vision devices during World War II. Since then, technology has advanced rapidly to include a variety of equipment, such as night vision goggles, thermal detection devices, infrared sniper scopes and telescopes.

The progress of night vision technology has been measured in generational sequence. Early optics using active infrared light were prone to malfunction. First-generation night vision devices were changed to passive infrared light and captured illumination from the moon and stars to augment reflected environmental infrared. With second-generation technology, images were amplified with intensifying tubes, but the ability to see in the lowest levels of light, such as on a moonless night, remained poor.

Third-generation night vision technology is the latest. While there is little improvement over the principles operating in second-generation gear, the most up-to-date equipment does provide sharper image resolution.

about two weeks and cover such important aspects of the art as fieldcraft and concealment, intelligence-gathering and basic survival skills.

Russell and Land were given the freedom to select the sniper recruits they wanted. Both were heavily influenced by Herbert McBride's chronicle of his sniping experience during World War I, *A Rifleman Went To War*. Land established his school on Hill 55 near Da Nang. One of Land's initial recruits was a friend, Gunnery Sergeant Carlos Hathcock, who had been a disenchanted MP in the Chu Lai area. Before the war, Hathcock had proven himself a champion marksman, winning numerous competitions. He was to emerge from the conflict a sniping legend.

As early as the autumn of 1965, Marine snipers were responding to the enemy menace. Three years later, the Marine sniper became official. Gilbert wrote, 'The success of the Marine sniping programme led to a formalization of the sniper's position within the Marine Corps structure. In June 1968, divisional orders approved the organization and formation of sniper platoons within each regiment's headquarters company and in the headquarters and service company of the reconnaissance battalion. The infantry regiment sniper platoon consisted of three squads of five two-man teams and a squad leader each, plus a senior NCO, an armourer and an officer, with a total strength of one officer and thirty-five enlisted men. The reconnaissance battalion had four squads of three two-man teams each under a squad leader, plus a senior NCO, armourer and officer, with a total strength of one officer and thirty enlisted men …'.

CHOICE OF WEAPONS

Captain Julian Ewell was the leading sniper advocate in the US Army. He formalized a sniper policy within the 9th Infantry Division, assigning six snipers to each

M-40A1

Country of Origin	United States
Calibre	7.62mm (0.30in)
Overall length	1117mm (44in)
Barrel length	610mm (24in)
Weight	6.57kg (14.48lb)

battalion and a pair at the brigade headquarters level. The M-14 rifle, upgraded with the M84 telescopic sight, was the preferred Army sniping weapon, and it could also be equipped with the Starlight night vision scope, usually effective to distances of 400m (437 yards).

On the other hand, the Marines chose the bolt-action Remington 700 rifle equipped with the M84 scope and designated it the M-4 after extensive testing of several rifles, including the M-14 and the Winchester Model 70, which was regularly chambered for 7.63mm (.30-06in) bullets rather than the NATO standard 7.62mm (0.30in) cartridge. At the same time, the lightweight M-16, capable of semiautomatic and automatic settings like the M-14, became the standard infantry weapon of the US Army. The M-16 fired a smaller 5.56mm (0.223in) calibre bullet, and it was not well suited to sniping. However, in *The Military Sniper Since 1914*, Martin Pegler notes one unusual circumstance. 'In desperation, a few men had commercial scopes mailed to them and persuaded unit armourers [to] fit them to M16s, with some success. One officer of the 25th Infantry Division had an impressive tally of 50 kills with a scoped M16 by the time he was shipped home in late 1966.'

HILL 55

Captain Land had been urged on with his effort at Hill 55 by Major General Herman Nickerson Jr, commander of the 1st Marine Division. 'I want mine [snipers] to be the best in the Marine Corps,' the commander said. 'I want them killing VC and I don't care how they do it – even if you have to go out and do it yourself,' reported Craig Roberts and Charles W. Sasser in their book *One Shot – One Kill*. Within a very short period of time, the deployment of snipers began to have a telling effect on the Viet Cong and the North Vietnamese Army.

The topography of Hill 55 resembled that of a hand with fingers emanating from it. For some time, a single Viet Cong sniper had played havoc with Marines who occupied the ridge called Finger One. 'Just within the past two weeks he had killed two Marines and wounded two others,' recalled Land in *One Shot – One Kill*. 'The grunts had been unable to locate his hide and eliminate him. Marines on the finger darted about like mice afraid to show themselves to a cat whose taloned paws were capable of swatting them at will.'

One of the first assignments for Marine snipers fell to Land himself and partner Sergeant Don Reinke – eliminate the menace to Finger One. The two went about gathering information on the sniper's victims, the trajectory of the shots which had killed or wounded Marines, the direction from which the shots had come. They also noticed the feeding habits of birds, which avoided a certain area near the hill. The pair conducted a reconnaissance which revealed that the sniper had made use of a 'tunnel' through tall grass after approaching the same hiding place from several directions over a number of days.

'Reinke and I worked our way back,' continued Land, '… careful to leave behind as few signs of our visit as possible. I had a plan.

'"See to the left of that brush pile where you can barely see the grass looks a little different?" I asked the platoon leader on the hill, pointing.

'"Yes, sir."

Below: Lance Corporal J.W. Howell observes enemy positions for his sniper partner, Corporal F.S. Sanders. These men of the 1st Marine Division were participating in Operation Swift in September 1967.

'"Bore-sight a 106 directly on that spot. We have no way of catching the sniper until he returns and fires a shot, but when he does – fire the recoilless …"

'The Marine swiveled the long 106-millimeter [4.1in] recoilless antitank weapon and deflected the barrel until its open snout pointed directly at the sniper's hide. The gunner slammed in an HE round and locked the breech. All he had to do was slap the push-button trigger …

'Late one afternoon a few days after the 106 was made ready, a shot rang out from the field. Fortunately, for one of the first times in his short-lived career, the gook sniper missed his target. The bullet gouged harmlessly into a sandbag inches behind a Marine who was darting across the open from one place to another.

'While grunts either dropped where they were or leaped into the nearest bunker, the 106 gunner dashed for his weapon. He made a headlong dive for the gun's sandbagged emplacement and hit the push button. The muzzle belched a stream of flame at the field; the rocketlike backblast exploded a cloud of dust.

'There was more than one way to get one shot – one kill.'

LONG-RANGE WONDER

Marine sniper Vaughn Nickell went after a Viet Cong sniper at Phu Loc on 6 January 1967, and registered the longest-range confirmed kill on record with the venerable M-1D rifle. Nickell dispatched his quarry at a range of slightly more than 1097m (1200 yards).

'The outpost was manned by a Company from 2nd Battalion 5th Marines,' reported author Ron Willoughby who was paired with Nickell, 'and the Company Commander's concern was that he had started to hear that some of the Marines were teasing Charlie and challenging him to shoot. The unfortunate thing was they didn't know where he was going to show up. And, the unfortunate thing for 6 o'clock Charlie was that after slightly wounding a teasing Marine in the back side, the Marines at Phu Loc 6 got their own Sniper team.

'Aside from other duties the sniper team of Ron Willoughby and Vaughn "Nick" Nickell would start to hunt Charlie each evening around 6pm, moving to different locations each night. One evening in mid January 1967, Ron had been called away briefly by the Company Commander. He left the Sniper weapon, an M1D, with Vaughn. When a call came from another location on the hill saying that they thought they saw Charlie, Vaughn grabbed the rifle and took off toward the location. Sure enough after looking through his scope (a 4power fixed scope), he saw 6 o'clock Charlie 1,100 meters [1202 yards] out positioning himself for the evening attack. Not having time to make any sight adjustments Vaughn got himself into a firing position. Using one of the Marines as a spotter he fired. The first shot was slightly to the left and about [91cm] 3 feet short. The second shot kicked up dirt right next to 6 o'clock Charlie. Now realizing that someone had him in his sight, Charlie started to make his move to get out of harm's way when the third shot rang out dropping Charlie in his tracks. It was an excellent 1,100 meter [1202-yard] shot on a cold rainy day by Vaughn Nickell at Phu Loc 6 using the M1D. Time of Charlie's death – 6 o'clock. Body and weapon recovered.'

M-21

Country of Origin	United States
Calibre	7.62mm (0.30in)
Overall length	1120mm (44.1in)
Barrel length	559mm (22in)
Weight	5.55kg (12.24lb)

'ONE SHOT – ONE KILL'

The most celebrated sniper of the Vietnam era was undoubtedly Carlos Hathcock. Hathcock had been acquainted with Captain Land prior to their deployment to Vietnam. The accomplished marksman had won the US 1000-Yard High Power Rifle championship in 1965, and he eventually became a sniper instructor and one of the architects of Marine sniper training in the post-Vietnam era.

'There can be little doubt that Gunnery Sergeant Hathcock was effective in his role as a sniper,' wrote Land in his foreword to Charles Henderson's book *Marine Sniper – 93 Confirmed Kills*. 'What is not widely known is that he became the focal point of a staff effort to legitimize sniping.

'I was the marksmanship co-ordinator in the Office of Training at Headquarters, United States Marine Corps, from 1975–1977. During this period we staffed a proposal for a permanent table of organization and table of equipment for the sniper unit.

'There was a strong effort at this time to delete the sniper program from the Marine Corps. As a result, I conducted a personal lobbying program that extended from the handball courts to the briefing rooms; from the Officer's Club at Quantico to seminars on urban warfare. There, Carlos became the symbol of what could be.

'Eventually, through the efforts of many men, a permanent sniper table of organization and table of equipment within every Marine Division was established, and approval was given for what has become the finest school on the art of sniping in the world. Without Hathcock's story and without his courage, perhaps none of this would have come to pass.'

Hathcock did score 93 confirmed kills during two tours in Vietnam, establishing a record for long-range sniping when he shot a Viet Cong weapons carrier from a distance of 2286m (2500 yards) with a telescopically sighted Browning M2 0.5in (12.7mm) machine gun set for a single shot. The North Vietnamese twice placed bounties on Hathcock's head, and they did so with other snipers as well.

Hathcock was also known to his enemies as 'Long Tra'ng' – 'White Feather'. On 16 September 1969, he was severely burned during an ambush and heroically helped remove several wounded Marines from their flaming amtrac. Hathcock died of multiple sclerosis in 1999, but his exploits remain some of the most incredible examples of patience, concentration and courage ever exhibited in wartime.

According to Henderson, a dozen well-trained enemy snipers once ventured southward in search of Long Tra'ng. Near Hill 55, Hathcock and Lance Corporal John Burke set out to do battle with one of them, nicknamed the Cobra, who had targeted several Marines in an attempt to draw his adversary into single combat.

'The sun lay low in the afternoon sky,' wrote Henderson, 'sending its light down the hill at Hathcock's and Burke's backs and casting long shadows across the wide, grass-covered gap that sloped toward the gully where two almond-shaped eyes squinted behind a pair of black binoculars.

'The enemy sniper slowly searched each tree trunk and bush for the white feather. "The arrogance of such a thing will cost this man his life", the sniper thought, as he picked apart the cover opposite him. "I will teach you to flaunt yourself. It is the humble man who wins here, my friend".

Below: *Using a telescopically sighted M-16 rifle, a US Marine sniper looks down range during training. The M-16 was one of many sniper rifles used by American troops in Vietnam.*

M-16 ARMALITE

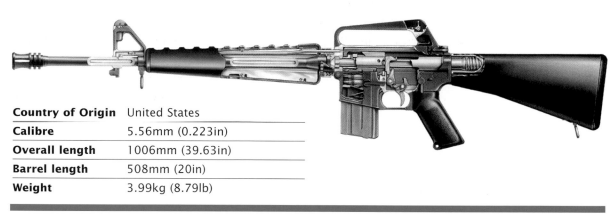

Country of Origin	United States
Calibre	5.56mm (0.223in)
Overall length	1006mm (39.63in)
Barrel length	508mm (20in)
Weight	3.99kg (8.79lb)

'As he trained his binoculars again at the top of the hill where the trees met the crest of the gap, something caught his eye, something small, yet bright, fluttering in the shadows. The little man squeezed his eyes shut and looked again through his binoculars, squinting to see through the blinding rays of the low sun. "I think, maybe, I have found you, my young warrior with the white plume".

'In a smooth and deliberate motion, the North Vietnamese sniper raised his rifle from the gully and tucked it into his shoulder, steadying it with his left hand, which he rested on the ground above the trench. He concentrated on the pointed sight-post inside the scope, but his target disappeared in the sun's glare, causing him to tilt and cant the weapon as he tried to pinpoint the Marine through the small scope and kill him.

'"What's that?" Hathcock said, catching a flash of light in his scope …

'"Hold tight, Burke. I'm gonna gamble a shot".

'Carefully, Hathcock centered his scope's reticle on the glimmer of reflected sunlight. He released his breath and let the cross hairs settle on the target, and, as they settled, his [7.63mm] .30-06 cracked down the hill, echoing through the wide, treeless gap …

'"Sergeant Hathcock! You got him", Burke said as the glimmer disappeared and revealed the now dead man whose body had bounded against the opposite side of the gully when the bullet struck.

'Hathcock smiled at his partner and said, "One shot – one kill" …

'Burke reached the body first. He looked at his sergeant and said, "Nobody is gonna believe this unless they see it.… You put the round straight through his scope!" …

'"Burke, I just had a scary thought. What's the only way a person could make a shot like this?"

'Burke looked puzzled. "What do you mean, Sergeant?"

'"Stop and think about it. He had to be sighting his rifle right at me in order for

my bullet to pass clean through his scope and get him in the eye like that."
"'Why, then he almost had you!'"

"'Yeah, Burke, when you get down to it, the only difference between me and him is I got on the trigger first'."

HIGH-VALUE TARGET

During another mission, Hathcock was airlifted to an area near the Laotian border. For over four days, he evaded detection by enemy patrols, some so close he could hear their conversations. He lay motionless for hours, advancing only inches at a time, bathed in his own sweat and bitten countless times by insects which would have driven an ordinary man to distraction.

On the morning of the fourth day, Hathcock was in position to deliver a single lethal rifle shot into his quarry, a North Vietnamese Army general. 'From somewhere behind the complex of bunkers came the sound of an automobile's engine,' wrote Henderson. 'The white sedan wheeled around the bunkers and stopped short of the walkway upon which Carlos held the rifle scope's cross hairs....

"'Here we go", Hathcock told himself. "Get a firm grip. Watch the cross hairs." The general stepped through the doorway, and Hathcock centered the man's profile in his scope. He waited for him to turn face-on. He did, but as the commander turned and walked toward the sniper's sight, the general's aide-de-camp stepped ahead of him. "Dummy! Don't you know that aides always walk to the left of their generals? Get out of the way!"

'Based on his estimations, he decided to place his scope's reticle on the general's left breast, in case the breeze carried the round [20.3cm] eight inches right. The bright sunlight warned the sniper to keep his aim high on the man's chest, but not too high, in case the heat raised the bullet's flight a few inches.

'The group of officers walking out with the general departed toward the side of the house. It left only the old man and his youthful aide. Carlos waited. The young officer took his place at the left side of his superior. Hathcock said, "Now stop." Both men did. The sniper's cross hairs lay directly on the general's heart.

'Hathcock's mind raced through all his marksmanship principles. "Good firm grip, watch the cross hairs, squeeze the trigger, wait for the recoil. Don't hold your breath too long, breathe and relax, let it come to the natural pause, watch the cross hairs, squeeeeeeeeeze."

'Recoil sent a jolt down his shoulder. He blinked and the general lay flat on his back. Blood gushed from the old officer's chest and his lifeless eyes stared into the sun's whiteness.'

KILLING MACHINE

In the year 2000, Tony Perry, a writer for the *Los Angeles Times*, interviewed 51-year-old Chuck Mawhinney, who years earlier had become the top-scoring Marine

Opposite: Wading through waist-deep water in a rice paddy, a US Marine patrol secures the perimeter around the strategically vital air base at Da Nang, South Vietnam, June 1965.

'At every moment since the sun rose Hathcock had refined his attunement to the environment ...'

Charles Henderson, Marine Sniper – 93 Confirmed Kills

sniper of the Vietnam War with 103 confirmed kills. Mawhinney is often asked to speak to military gatherings, particularly at the Marine Corps sniper school at Camp Pendleton, California, or the Army school at Fort Carson, Colorado. Mawhinney had not sought the limelight, but the retired former employee of the US Forest Service revealed numerous aspects of his 16 months as a sniper in Vietnam. 'I never looked in their eyes, I never stopped to think about whether the guy had a wife or kids,' he told Perry.

'... As a sniper, Mawhinney had an uncanny ability to gauge distance, moisture, weather and terrain – factors that determine how much a bullet will rise or drop during flight. He had the patience to wait for hours for the right shot. 'He was scared but exhilarated,' the reporter wrote.

'"Normally I would shoot and run, but if I had them at a [long] distance, I wasn't worried", Mawhinney said. "I would shoot and then lay there and wait and wait and wait and pretty soon somebody else would start moving toward the body. Then I would shoot again."'

'Near the An Hoa base outside Da Nang,' wrote Perry, 'he caught a platoon of North Vietnamese army regulars crossing a stream. He hit 16 with head shots with an M-14, which he often carried in addition to his bolt-action.

'The 16 were listed only as probable kills because no officer was there to see the lifeless bodies float by and there was no chance to search the bodies.'

HEIGHTENED SENSATIONS

'"When you fire, your senses start going into overtime: eyes, ears, smell, everything", he said. "Your vision widens out so you see everything, and you can smell things like you can't at other times. My rules of engagement were simple: If they had a weapon, they were going down. Except for an NVA paymaster I hit at [823m] 900 yards, everyone I killed had a weapon".'

Chuck Mawhinney, Marine Corps sniper, as reported by the *Los Angeles Times*

TOP GUN

The top-scoring American sniper of the Vietnam War, with 113 confirmed kills, was Sergeant Adelbert F. Waldron of the Army's 9th Infantry Division. In *Sniper*, Adrian Gilbert relates that Waldron was once aboard a small boat gliding down the Mekong River. He shot a troublesome sniper from the top of a coconut tree 900m (823 yards) away, while the boat was moving!

In *Stalk and Kill: The Sniper Experience*, Gilbert related the contents of an official report detailing another example of Waldron's skill. 'Sergeant Waldron and his partner occupied a night ambush position with Company D, 3/60th Infantry on 4 February 1969 approximately three kilometres [1.8 miles] south of Ben Tre. The area selected for the ambush was at the end of a large rice paddy adjacent to a wooded area. Company D, 3/60th Infantry had conducted a MEDCAP and ICAP ... during the day, hoping to gain information on Viet Cong movements in the area.

'At approximately 2105 hours, five Viet Cong moved from the wooded area towards Sergeant Waldron's position and he took the first one in the group under fire, resulting in one Viet Cong killed. The remaining Viet Cong immediately dropped to the ground and did not move for several minutes. A short time later, the four Viet Cong stood up and began moving again, apparently not aware they were being fired upon from the rice paddy. Sergeant Waldron took the four Viet Cong under fire, resulting in four Viet Cong killed.

'The next contact took place at 2345 hours, when four Viet Cong moved into the rice paddy from the left of Sergeant Waldron's ambush position. The Viet Cong were taken under fire by Sergeant Waldron, resulting in four Viet Cong killed. A total of nine enemy soldiers were killed during the night at an average range of 400 metres [437 yards]. Sergeant Waldron used a Starlight Scope and noise suppressor on his match-grade M14 rifle in obtaining these kills.'

Using shallow-draft river-going vessels which were heavily armed to engage enemy forces along the banks, the US Navy prosecuted a unique war in Vietnam. The operations of the 'Brown Water Navy' were often coordinated with units of the American or South Vietnamese armies. Some of the Mobile Riverine Force's (MRF) offensive forays were also carried out at night. A once classified report of nocturnal MRF operations in March 1969, describes an illuminating addition.

Below: *From his position behind a brick wall, a US Marine sniper searches through the Redfield telescopic sight affixed to his M-40 rifle.*

Above: *In June 1969,*
Deputy Secretary of
Defense David Packard
handles a sniper-scoped
M-16 rifle at Holmdahl
Hill as Lieutenant
Colonel Frank Oblinger
of the 2nd Infantry
Division watches.

'A recent innovation, utilized in MRF night operations is the searchlight (pinkeye) boat. Since enemy forces frequently move under cover of darkness, a method to enhance the effectiveness of night operations was developed. A [58.4cm] 23-inch XENON tank searchlight, modified with a pink filter to provide compatibility with a starlight scope, was mounted on the flight deck of ATC-131-13. The recognition range of this apparatus has been demonstrated to be up to 2000 meters [2187 yards]. Two to four Army snipers are positioned on the flight deck as the ATC cruises 100–200 meters [109–219 yards] offshore. A 105-mm [4.1in] howitzer equipped to monitor may operate with the "pinkeye" boat ready to fire beehive rounds on enemy troops marked by sniper tracers.

'During the period late February to 21 March, 24 Viet Cong have been killed by "pinkeye" snipers. Although still in the developmental state, this equipment shows potential for application in interdiction operations. At 0017 on 15 March, "pinkeye" with 3/60th Infantry Division snipers aboard in company with M-151-1 spotted six to ten Viet Cong in a restricted area, [3.2km] 2 miles south-southeast of Dong Tam. Snipers marked the position with tracers and the monitor fired 105-mm [4.1in] beehive into the area resulting in three Viet Cong killed by snipers and three killed (probable) by beehive. After midnight on 21 March the "pinkeye" with two sniper teams aboard killed eight Viet Cong in a restricted area on the south bank of the My Tho … The successful employment of snipers on river assault craft has led to an arrangement for Navy personnel to be sniper trained.'

Despite the horrors of war, armed conflict remains a dreaded facet of the human condition. Although the sniper may be loathed and lauded at the same time, his value was proven in Vietnam. Modern armies train their snipers as elite soldiers, and their deployment to the battlefield is now a foregone conclusion. Warfare was increasingly refined throughout the twentieth century. Technology accounted for ever-growing numbers of casualties. With the advent of automatic weapons, the rank-and-file soldier expended more and more ammunition in order to account for an enemy killed or wounded. During World War I, the estimate had been roughly 7000 rounds per casualty. The estimate for World War II was raised to 25,000 rounds. In Vietnam, some figures exceeded 50,000 rounds per enemy killed or wounded. Conversely, the sniper, very often employing a lower-tech instrument of destruction, proved to be an efficient killer. Estimates of his bullet-to-casualty ratio run as low as 1.3 rounds per wounded or dead adversary. The cost of the single bullet? Something under 20 cents.

FIRST KILL

Snipers of the Vietnam era faced the same conflicting emotions and varied responses from fellow soldiers as those in earlier wars. To this day, some of them carry mental images of their enemies. Mawhinney, for example, still remembers one Viet Cong, dressed in the familiar pajamas, who eluded several shots from his rifle. An armourer had undoubtedly altered the settings of his scope. Gilbert described the first kill by Marine Corporal Jerry Clifford, a scout-sniper of Charlie Company 1/1, which forever changed the young man's definition of war.

'The Hill 55 area was mostly flat with a few rolling hills. I guess a first kill is always an unforgettable experience. I certainly will never forget mine. "She" was about eighteen and was carrying an M1 carbine. At the time I did not know that he was a "she", and, of course, I did not know she was pregnant. The shot was overlooking a free-fire zone (which was a slightly elevated plateau) outside a deserted villa. A small VC patrol broke from the tree line and was re-entering it when I took out "tail-end Charlie". The shot was about [549m] 600 yards, through the lower back and out the front. The body and rifle were recovered, the kill confirmed. The grunts gave me credit for "two with one shot". I took solace in staring at the sun.'

In the war-torn city of Sarajevo, Bosnia, a NATO peacekeeping French Foreign Legion counter-sniper team, armed with a Harris (McMillan) M87R .50-calibre (12.7mm) sniper rifle, keeps lookout from on high for potential aggressors. A multinational force has been deployed in Bosnia since the early 1990s.

CHAPTER EIGHT

PARAMILITARY SNIPERS

Freedom fighter, terrorist or mercenary, he deals death from a distant window or darkened alley. Often with little or no formal training, following a charismatic leader or dedicated to a revolutionary purpose, the paramilitary sniper has many faces — each of them lethal.

The crowded streets of Mogadishu had been transformed into an urban killing zone. Machine guns rattled, rocket-propelled grenades hissed into walls, and shuddering explosions rocked the centre of the capital city of war-torn Somalia. Assigned to capture Somali warlord Mohamed Farah Aideed and a number of other thugs, the soldiers of Task Force Ranger deployed on the afternoon of 3 October 1993. Since August, they had conducted half a dozen such lightning raids. This time, however, the 200 fighting men of the 3rd Battalion, 75th Rangers, the 10th Mountain Division, the 160th Special Operations Aviation Regiment, Delta Force, Navy SEAL snipers, and special tactics troops found themselves in a fight for their lives.

Two Army Blackhawk helicopters went down during the pitched battle, and a pair of Delta Force snipers, Master Sergeant Gary Gordon and Sergeant First Class Randy Shughart, requested permission to come to the aid of one of the downed crews.

Permission was initially denied, but a second request was approved, and the two roped down from their hovering Blackhawk into the teeth of a raging, heavily armed mob. Gordon and Shughart moved more than 100m (109 yards) to the downed helicopter and pulled the crewmen to temporary safety. Between them, the two snipers coolly and methodically killed or wounded an estimated 100 Somalis before losing their lives. Both men were posthumously awarded the Congressional Medal of Honor for their heroic sacrifice. During the engagement, 18 Rangers were killed and 73 wounded. Aideed escaped but was killed during fighting three years later.

In their book *No Room For Error: The Covert Operations of America's Special Tactics Units From Iran to Afghanistan*, authors Benjamin F. Schemmer and Colonel John T. Carney Jr estimate that 500 Somalis were killed in the fighting that day and that up to 1000 were wounded. American forces subsequently withdrew from Somalia as political pressure dictated the direction of military operations. Although the foray into Somalia had been bitter, the fighting ability of the US military was never questioned.

TERRORIST SNIPERS

Since World War II, and indeed throughout modern military history, the armed forces of numerous nations have faced paramilitary organizations led by warlords, anarchists, political activists and demagogues. Freedom fighters to some and armed thugs to others, these paramilitary groups have employed the sniper as a weapon of terror and a means of demoralizing peacekeepers and interdicting troops. At any given time during the latter half of the twentieth century, unrest has found troops from the United States, Great Britain, Russia and numerous other countries, sometimes sponsored by the United Nations (UN) or the North Atlantic Treaty Organization (NATO), in the field confronting unstable situations.

In 1969, the British Army was drawn into the conflict between Protestant and Catholic factions in Northern Ireland. Although their mission was initially to restore order, the British were soon in conflict with the militant Irish Republican Army

Below: Alert for Irish Republican Army (IRA) militants, a sniper team from British 40 Commando surveys a section of Belfast, Northern Ireland, from a neighbourhood rooftop, 1 August 1972.

Left: *From a dark
doorway in rural
Northern Ireland, a
hooded member of the
IRA aims his M-16
Armalite rifle for the
benefit of the camera.*

(IRA), the principal group conducting terrorist operations in the area. IRA snipers were often able to secrete themselves in windows and on rooftops, or along country roads, ambushing British patrols and then slipping away into a labyrinth of houses or even across the border into the neighbouring Republic of Ireland.

In *Stalk and Kill: The Sniper Experience*, Adrian Gilbert relates one harrowing encounter. 'Patrolling the streets of Belfast or Londonderry, the security forces were vulnerable to terrorist gunmen. Many of these were merely IRA "cowboys" taking pot shots at the British, but others were more competent. A sergeant in the Royal Green Jackets noted the activities of one such terrorist: "We had a guy killed and two others injured by a single shot through the back window of a Saracen [armoured vehicle]. The round passed through the head of the first man, killing him outright, took out an eye and damaged the nose of the second bloke, and ended up in the third guy's ass. The gunman had lain down on the table in the back kitchen of a house they'd taken over, propped up the letter box with a pencil and fired through the whole length of the house, out of the door and into the back of the passing vehicle. It was either a very lucky shot, or the gunman was very good. The Belfast IRA had a guy we nicknamed 'One-shot Willy' working for them at the time, and we always reckoned he might have done it".'

David Ash commanded a platoon of the 1st Battalion, The Light Infantry, and kept a diary of events in Northern Ireland. On 8 August 1972, he recorded, 'We were out on daylight foot patrols in the Ardoyne yesterday. Pte Pearson got a bullet in the

Below: *A British soldier demonstrates a new night sight, used for the first time in action in February 1973, in the New Lodge Road area of Belfast, Northern Ireland. He is armed with the standard British rifle of the period, the L1A1 Self-Loading Rifle (SLR).*

thigh, my first casualty. IRA snipers are clearly still at work in the area, or perhaps whole units are slowly returning to resume operations … Yesterday, I was patrolling south with a section through the waste ground between Etna Drive and Jamaica Street … Shots rang out somewhere ahead of me; the unmistakable Crack! Crack! Crack! of high velocity shots. But in these streets it's impossible to tell where the shooting is coming from … It was fairly obvious the gunman was ahead of me on this occasion, and probably firing at Sgt. Spracklen's patrol … I raced across Etna Drive to the location. The shooting stopped. Young Pearson lay in a front garden, combat trousers dark red with wet blood.'

The close proximity of the civilian population and the danger of killing or wounding innocent people compounded the problem of dealing with a determined IRA sniper. The most effective response to terror sniping proved to be the well-trained military shooter functioning in a counter-sniper role. In October 1972, Ash witnessed an effective response to incoming IRA fire. 'Pte Mahony took cover behind Young's burnt out garage. He climbed onto the flat roof and settled into a fire position with his sniper scope. The IRA was quick to spot him. Patterns of red brick dust erupted around him as bursts of fire were directed at him. He began returning fire, just steady, aimed shots. A very cool young man.'

Gilbert reports the nocturnal experience of one Royal Marine sniper from 40 Commando. 'We had only brought our L42s [sniper rifles] with us and one IWS [night sight]; we also had no binos, so we used the 32 scope on the rifles for observation. As it got dark we found out one of the major problems with the IWS. After looking through it, one is blind in that eye for a few seconds afterwards. You were supposed to observe through the non-shooting eye but that was often impractical … As the SLR [self-loading rifle] was fired,

THE LEBANON

In early 1983, US Marines were deployed to the Middle Eastern nation of Lebanon, which was wracked by civil war during and after the withdrawal of Israeli forces which had attacked strongholds of the Palestine Liberation Organization the previous year. Numerous Christian and Muslim factions battled in the streets of Beirut, the Lebanese capital, and in October 1983, the Marines became a terrorist target. A truck bomb exploded as the vehicle was driven into a barracks, killing 243 US personnel.

The Marines were initially required to abide by strict rules of engagement; however, when the authorization to shoot back was received Corporal Tom Rutter and a fellow Marine offered a rude surprise to the Shiite militia who had chewed at their position with a heavy machine gun.

'I concentrated through sweat on the shattered city as I swept my cross hairs across it,' Rutter told Charles W. Sasser and Craig Roberts in *One Shot – One Kill.* 'I stopped when I saw a muzzle flash blossom from the darkened revetment of a sandbagged bunker at a street intersection. The bunker's firing port was a rectangle about [15.2cm by 30.4cm] six inches by a foot in width. I waited until the muzzle flashed in it again before I sent a single [11.2g] 173-grain bullet through the tiny opening ...

'While I was busy with the bunker, [Corporal Jon] Crumley was still playing cat-and-mouse with the raghead behind the berm... He had made a mistake in establishing a predictable pattern. First, he fired from one end of the berm, then ran to the other end to fire ... Crumley zeroed in his scope at the berm's near end and waited...

'"He's mine," Crumley announced calmly while I watched through my scope.

'"He's yours."

'The skirmisher was wearing a patterned turban. He stuck it and his head up once too often. Crumley was ready. He fired. The high-powered bullet kicked up dirt in front of the man's face. At the same time, his face underneath the turban literally exploded.'

the figure of a man came sprinting round the corner from Carlisle Circus and stood pressed to the wall looking around the way he had come, with a pistol in his hand held up in classic James Bond style ... I almost threw the IWS down and put the L42 to my shoulder. It was not a good position to fire from, and as I had been squinting through the IWS, when I put the scope to my eye I couldn't see.

'I stayed on aim and gradually I got my vision back; this only took a few seconds but it seemed like an eternity. The man had changed position to what I think was a doorway, and I put the pointer of the sight on his chest and squeezed off a shot. I quickly reloaded and came back on aim but he had simply disappeared. We both thought he might have gone to ground, so we emptied our magazines into all the likely shadows and the ground where we had seen him ... I was convinced I had missed the guy ... However, towards the end of the tour the unit 2i/c interviewed me. He had a list of, I believe, fifty-six names of terrorists shot by the unit, and after a short conversation put my name next to that of a man who had been found shot dead with a wound through the chest.'

Sporadic sniper incidents continued into the 1990s, and those who served in Northern Ireland remember the imminent danger of patrolling in a 'sniper's alley'.

DRUGS AND GUNS

According to a September 2003 report by David Adams of the *St. Petersburg Times*, the city of Medellin, Colombia, has actually become a safer place within the last year. Long known as the hometown of perhaps the most feared drug cartel in the world, Medellin had been synonymous with the trade.

'... From his commanding position atop a hill overlooking the poor barrios that line the western slopes of Colombia's second-largest city, police Capt. Reynaldo Reyes recalled how barely a year ago his officers could not set foot here. '"Down there were the guerrilla trenches," he said, pointing to a line of shabby, single-story brick homes. "They had snipers in every building ..." Last year, 3443 killings were reported in the greater Medellin area ...

'Since then, the situation has changed dramatically. Police and army soldiers control the area, known as "Comuna 13", and crime has plummeted in the last year. Colombian officials say Medellin, once considered one of the world's murder capitals, is a more peaceful city ...

'But imposing law and order has not been easy, especially in tough areas like Comuna 13. In October, government forces entered Comuna 13 by force. Code-named "Operation Orion", hundreds of heavily armed police and soldiers fought their way into the neighborhood, engaging in pitched battles with the guerrillas. By the time government forces had retaken control, 19 police and soldiers were dead, as were 25 guerrillas. Some 400 people were arrested and dozens of weapons and explosives seized.'

> **'Down there were the guerrilla trenches. They had snipers in every building.'**
>
> *Captain Reynaldo Reyes of the Medellin police, Colombia*

THE BALKANS

With the Bosnian declaration of sovereignty in October 1991, a civil war erupted in the Balkans, a flashpoint for violence over the centuries. Supported by the government of neighbouring Serbia, many Serbs who were living in Bosnia rose up in the wake of a referendum on independence from Yugoslavia. On 21 November 1995, the Dayton Agreement finally divided Bosnia and Herzegovina between two political entities, the Republika Srpska, dominated by the Bosnian Serbs, and the Federation of Bosnia and Herzegovina.

The city of Sarajevo, now officially part of Bosnia and Herzegovina, was besieged by the warring factions from the spring of 1992 until the siege was officially declared over on 29 February 1996. During that time, Sarajevo was a killing ground of sniper alleys. An estimated 5000 people died in the fighting, and during one horrendous day, 22 July 1993, a total of 3777 artillery shells struck the shattered city. UN-sponsored peacekeepers moved into Sarajevo armed with sophisticated counter-sniping equipment, including the latest in telescopic sights and machine

His identity concealed with a ski mask, a drug gang member stands watch in the streets of Medellin, Colombia, August, 2000. Reclaiming the area has been a police priority.

ISRAEL AND PALESTINE

The tinderbox of the Middle East continues to be the scene of fighting between soldiers of the Israel Defense Forces and guerrillas of the Palestine Liberation Organization, Hamas and other paramilitary groups. Amid charge and countercharge, each side asserts that the barbarity of the other contributes to the escalating violence. An Associated Press report in October 1996 quoted the Israeli newspaper *Yediot Aharonot* as saying Palestinian Authority leader Yasser Arafat had ordered snipers to provoke fighting. 'Snipers were located, among other places, at the main Israel–Gaza crossing point, where Palestinian police covered them during four hours of clashes there. The sharpshooters' fire was pre-planned, and done with orders from above. These were actions that were well planned and were prepared even before the violence broke out.' Some of the Palestinians firing on Israeli positions were sharpshooters with telescopic sights, who were shooting with the intent to kill, related an Israeli television commentator who alluded to investigations by the Israeli Army.

Six years later, Israeli soldiers had Arafat holed up in his headquarters. 'The Palestinian leader has been besieged for 17 days with about 100 to 200 followers, including soldiers and armed security guards, administrative staff and a handful of journalists and medical personnel,' noted a *Washington Post* News Service story. 'Israeli snipers are less than [27.4m] 30 yards from the Palestinian gunmen who peer out of the building through dirty blinds ...'

Arafat remains the leader of the Palestinian Authority, but Israeli forces are aggressively targeting the leaders of guerrilla factions.

guns. The multinational peacekeepers kept watch on the hills surrounding the city, recording the locations of sniper nests and calling upon their firepower, which was capable of delivering suppressing fire against marauding Serb snipers within a matter of seconds, finally helping to break the siege.

The Bosnia Action Coalition released a weekly report on events in Bosnia and Herzegovina. Its 7 March 1995 statement recorded a litany of atrocities committed by Serb snipers.

'A 24-year-old Sarajevan was murdered by Serb snipers Friday and 13 others were wounded last week, including an 11-year-old boy,' it reads. 'Yesterday, a Serb sharpshooter killed a 60-year-old man on the outskirts of Sarajevo as he worked in his garden; another man and a 14-year-old boy were wounded while in the city center. A 34-year-old woman in Dobrinja was shot in the back by a Serb sniper as she played with her children Friday, Reuters reports. Also Friday, a 20-year-old man was shot as he walked in Sarajevo center; the bullet damaged his spinal cord, and he is now paralyzed. Two passengers were wounded when Serbs fired at a tram Friday from snipers' nests near the city's Vrbanja bridge, UN officers said.

'The UN "does not have words strong enough to condemn such attacks," said spokesman Colum Murphy. However, it has taken little action to stop them. On Monday, the UN urged "both sides" to respect anti-sniping agreements although

UN officers admit the shooting is coming from Serb-held positions. AP reports French "peacekeepers" returned fire after snipers shot toward UN soldiers.... Sarajevo's civilians, however, must walk the streets without such protection.'

FRIEND OR FOE?

On 1 August 1995, *The New York Times* reported on an odd twist in the efforts to end indiscriminate sniping in Sarajevo. French forces, often equipped with the bolt action 7.62mm (0.30in) FR–F2 sniper rifle based on the MAS36 design, were apparently confronted by snipers of the Bosnian Army, rather than the Serbs.

'French peacekeeping troops in the United Nations unit trying to curtail Bosnian Serb sniping at civilians in Sarajevo have concluded that until mid-June some gunfire also came from Government soldiers deliberately shooting at their own civilians,' said the *Times*. 'After what was called a "definitive" investigation, a French marine unit that patrols against snipers said it traced sniper flares to a building normally occupied by Bosnian soldiers and other security forces.

'They say the sniper fire from the Government position stopped in mid-June, when, after several months of suspicion that the building was being used by snipers, a gunman was seen firing from the building. The officers say they notified the Bosnian Army that the sniper was about to be shot by French troops, as they are authorized to do. "We were going to kill him just as we shoot Serbian snipers," said

Below: Supporting NATO operations in the former Yugoslavia, a sniper from the 2nd Battalion, the Parachute Regiment, covers a colleague at a checkpoint using a L115A1 8.59mm (.338in) sniper rifle.

a French officer involved in the investigation. The Bosnian Army protested that it knew nothing about the gunman, but firing from the building immediately stopped, the officer said.'

The French anti-sniping team monitored the area for a week with one armoured vehicle near buildings known to be used by Bosnian Serb snipers. Other vehicles were secretly placed near the Parliament building. During the following week, the Serb positions were quiet a number of times when bullets were flying from the Parliament building. When a UN armoured personnel carrier was positioned in plain view of the Parliament building for several hours on three successive days, no sniper activity was reported in the area being monitored. When the vehicle was removed, the sniping resumed.

'Finally, the French said, they began to examine the building with what they described as very sophisticated optical enhancement devices that they have only recently received. That was when the gunman was seen, they said. Though they said they do not keep records of victims of snipers, the marines said they recall at least two civilians who were hit by bullets they believe were fired from the former Parliament building during their investigation …'

DEAD ZONE

Advancing technology will undoubtedly make a sniper's efforts to conceal his position progressively more difficult, and eventually maybe impossible. Thermal equipment detects the change in body temperature of an adversary, whose camouflage may be perfect. However, on a dark night, that temperature change will cause him to literally glow in the dark.

Still, the terror and the killing will continue. Reporting on 16 February 1996, Cameron McWhirter of the *Cincinnati Enquirer* captured the feeling of dread in the civilian population of Grbavica, a Bosnian neighbourhood gripped by fear during a period of uncertainty following the signing of the Dayton Agreement.

'The rooms of the bombed out apartment building appeared to have been occupied by snipers,' McWhirter wrote. 'The shattered windows provided a commanding view of the Bosnian government-held section of Sarajevo. The floor was littered with high-caliber shell casings ... To Serbs living here, Grbavica has become a dead zone. A Serbian stronghold throughout the four-year war, the neighborhood now is set to be turned over to the Muslim-backed government. "People are just really scared," said Sandra Djuric, 15 … "They don't feel safe now. They don't believe the Muslim government will protect them. Most of the people who can are leaving for the mountains".'

PARLIAMENTARY SNIPING

'Members of the United Nations anti-sniping unit, who said they are equipped with infrared and thermal viewing devices to watch suspected snipers' nests, said they began their investigation after studying the trajectory of bullets striking near central Sarajevo. They concluded that some of the shooting was coming from the former Parliament building. "It was the only place where some of the snipers could be," said a soldier on the investigating team ...'

New York Times, 1 August 1995

The province of Kosovo, part of southern Serbia, has also been the scene of Balkan strife as ethnic Albanians have fought Serbian authorities in a struggle for independence. The Serbian government reacted brutally to the threat, and eventually was at war with NATO forces. US Intelligence gathered reports of Serbian atrocities against Albanian civilians in Kosovo, including the ubiquitous terror-dealing sniper, who targeted military personnel and civilians alike. The sniper menace in Kosovo reached such a level that farmers were unable to harvest their crops or tend their livestock. As the number of US troops participating in the NATO operation swelled to several thousand, run-ins with Serbian paramilitary fighters were common.

Writing for the Armed Forces Press Service, Jim Garamone related, 'Rogue elements targeted US service members during two violent acts in Kosovo ... In the most serious incident, Serb snipers opened fire on Marines manning a roadblock in the village of Zegra, south of the Marine headquarters in Gnjilane. Marines killed one sniper and wounded two others. None of the 26th Marine Expeditionary Unit

Above: *From the twentieth floor of a Sarajevo apartment building, a Bosnian sniper watches for movement below through the site on his Dragunov SVD sniper rifle. Snipers were responsible for thousands of civilian casualties during four years of fighting.*

Above: *A sniper's view above the Bosnian city of Sarajevo. The many-storied apartment blocks in the cities of the former Yugoslavia made ideal hideouts for paramilitary snipers, who could fire from hidden, elevated positions before quickly moving to another part of the building to avoid detection.*

service members were hurt in the incident. In the second incident, snipers fired on 82nd Airborne soldiers near the US sector headquarters in Urosevac. US soldiers were able to detain two men ...

'"The biggest challenge facing US forces in Kosovo is a 'rogue element' that doesn't know about the military technical agreement or refuses to abide by the agreement," [Army Brigadier General John] Craddock said. "We still continue to find illegal checkpoints that we have to challenge. We have to disarm those people that are [manning] those checkpoints and we have to tear them down".'

On 14 February 2000, Jonathan Steele filed a report for *The Guardian*, which proved that Kosovo was still a very dangerous place – even as troops from France, Great Britain, Germany, Belgium and Italy moved into the town of Mitrovice to try to keep order.

'Snipers hiding in high-rise flats wounded two French soldiers in the divided Kosovan city of Mitrovice yesterday in defiance of a security clampdown by K-For, the NATO-led peace force. The ominous appearance of snipers and the targeting of K-For sent tension soaring in a city symbolising ethnic polarisation ... K-For troops fired back, killing one sniper and capturing two – Albanian men who had crossed the river from the southern side. Lieutenant Colonel Patrique Chanliau said a

French soldier was shot in the stomach while on patrol in the Serb part of the city. A second peacekeeper was shot in the arm after NATO troops launched a counter-attack on the snipers.'

CHECHNYA

Russian forces are grappling even now with paramilitary and terrorist elements in Chechnya. Having fought the Chechen rebels from 1992 to 1996, they withdrew to re-evaluate their operational tactics.

'The wars in Chechnya emphasized the value of snipers,' wrote Lester W. Grau and Charles Q. Cutshaw for *Infantry* magazine. 'The Chechens met the Russians in urban combat in Grozny and soon Chechen snipers took a toll on Russian forces. The stationary combat fought from ruined buildings resembled the fighting at Stalingrad. This time, however, the Russian "snipers" were at a disadvantage. They were trained to fight as part of an attacking combined-arms team that would advance rapidly against a conventional defending force. The Russian snipers were not prepared to hunt in the ruins and to lie in ambush for days on end. The Chechens, on the other hand, knew the territory and had plenty of sniper weapons.'

Below: Through the telescopic sight of an L115A1 8.59mm (.338in) Long Range Accuracy International sniper rifle, British paras with the NATO contingent in Macedonia are seen searching a house, 2001.

According to Grau and Cutshaw, the Russians had left behind 533 SVD sniper rifles when they had originally departed Chechnya. Soon, the Chechens had formed four-man teams, armed with an RPG, an SVD, and probably an assault rifle, as well as arming individual snipers with the SVD.

Below: Armed with a tripod-mounted heavy machine gun equipped with a telescopic sight, a Russian soldier prepares to attack Chechen fighter positions outside the city of Hasavyurt, Dagestan, close to the Chechen border, September 1999. For years, the breakaway province has seen bitter fighting that has left tens of thousands dead.

'Once the fighting moved beyond the cities and into the mountains,' they continued, 'Chechen snipers attempted to engage Russian forces at long distances – 900 to 1000 meters [984 to 1093 yards] away, although terrain and vegetation often limited their engagement ranges. Away from the cities, a Chechen sniper usually operated as part of a team – the sniper plus a four-man support element … The sniper would fire one or two shots at the Russians and then change firing positions. Should the Russians fire at the sniper, the support element would open fire at random to draw fire on itself and allow the sniper to escape.'

The Russians had not been prepared for the stealth and coordination of the Chechen snipers, and when they re-entered Chechnya in 1999, they too had formed 'hunter-killer' groups of two or three men. 'Aside from the TO&E military snipers who were employed as marksmen, the war in Chechnya saw the return of the elite sniper who was part of the government special reserves and hunted Chechens. These snipers avoid carrying their weapons in public since they do not want the locals to

DRAGUNOV SVD

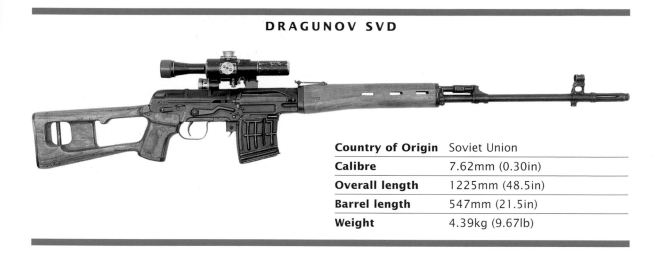

Country of Origin	Soviet Union
Calibre	7.62mm (0.30in)
Overall length	1225mm (48.5in)
Barrel length	547mm (21.5in)
Weight	4.39kg (9.67lb)

identify them as part of the sniper elite force. The sniper works as part of a team – two snipers plus a five-man security element armed with Kalashnikov assault rifles.'

The snipers take their positions at night, said the authors, but prepare them during daylight hours. The sniper pair is separated to cover an ambush area up to 300m (328 yards) distant, and the support element sets up to the rear and side. The elite Russian snipers are not members of the special operations units of the MVD (Ministry of the Interior) or FSB (the successor to the KGB). They are extended-service contract personnel and company-grade officers, some of whom participated in the war with the Mujahideen in Afghanistan during the 1980s, said Grau and Cutshaw.

'The battle for Grozny taught the Russians about the importance of snipers in an urban environment,' wrote First Lieutenant James Reed for the US Foreign Military Studies Office. 'Chechen snipers, at times only one or two single snipers, completely pinned down Russian units. In future urban operations, expect to see greater numbers of Russian snipers put into action in both sniper and countersniper roles.'

One American officer, when asked to comment on his nation's military operations around the world, described hostile elements taking cover among a civilian population and the threatening posture of paramilitary forces often encountered in areas of disturbance. At times such as these, he remarked, there is a great need for surgical rifle fire. The officer recalled an incident in Sierra Leone, when rebels had been warned to stay clear of Marine positions and the US embassy. One rebel leader brandished an automatic weapon, approached too closely and was dropped by a Marine sniper. This single demonstration of resolute, accurate fire defused a situation which had been potentially much more volatile.

In modern conflicts, the sniper is both peacekeeper and menace, lawman and provocateur. A lethal enemy and a welcome ally, he has become a necessity among the major armed forces of the world. Those who ignore the sniper and go into battle unprepared are likely to re-evaluate their tactical preparedness – and quickly.

A British sniper of the 3rd Battalion, the Parachute Regiment, takes up a position in the town of Basra, southern Iraq, April 2003. A large portrait of deposed president Saddam Hussein looms overhead, reminding the inhabitants of the formerly all-pervading influence of the Iraqi dictator.

CHAPTER NINE

RECENT CONFLICTS

Advanced technology has not displaced the sniper from today's battlefield. Steely nerve is only made more deadly by state-of-the-art equipment and the most recent generation of accurate weaponry. The battlefield of the future will likely remain the hunting ground of the sniper.

While the twentieth century may indeed be considered the most violent in human history, the character of that violence was varied and often confusing.

Two world wars had cost millions of lives, pitting organized armies against one another on battlefields which were both expansive and confined. Conflicts in Korea and Vietnam had been precipitated by an effort to contain the advance of Communism. The end of empire found civil war and unrest in many nations of the newly emerging Third World, and aggressive war was waged by despots. The global threat of terrorism had reached new heights during the last 50 years of the twentieth century and prompted the organized military machinery of numerous nations to respond with force.

Sadly, the dawn of the new millennium has seen a continuation of armed conflict in many regions. Regardless of the cause or catalyst, ideological, geopolitical, or nationalistic fervour, the sniper has performed his numerous functions during each

resulting engagement. Whether the enemy is a professional and well-trained opposing army or a shadowy, paramilitary merchant of terror, the sniper responds to the call of duty.

THE FALKLANDS WAR

When the military junta which governed the South American nation of Argentina launched an invasion of the Falkland Islands in April 1982, the British government reacted swiftly to reclaim its territory. A long dispute over the ownership of the islands off the coast of South America was sparked into armed conflict by the Argentine government, in part to divert public attention from a rapidly deteriorating economic situation.

As British troops deployed thousands of miles to the Falklands, sniper training was actually conducted aboard ship in many cases. According to Adrian Gilbert in *Stalk and Kill: The Sniper Experience*, the training was necessary once again due to a lack of ongoing preparedness. Snipers were utilized by both sides, and much of the fighting took place at night. Argentine snipers were usually equipped with the telescopically sighted Mauser-designed K98K, manufactured in their own country, although some used the US-made M-14 and a collection of other arms. British snipers were primarily armed with the L42A1 rifle, which had been introduced in the decade following World War II as a successful conversion of the old No. 4 Mk I (T) rifle from 7.7mm (0.303in) calibre ammunition to the NATO 7.62mm (0.30in) round.

'Argentinian troops were well equipped with night sights, mainly second-generation models such as the AN/PVS-4, which were superior to the first-generation Starlight scopes used by the British', wrote Gilbert.

Many of the British snipers were trained by David Cooper, described by Gilbert as a shooting enthusiast who also served as the padre of 2 Para, one of two battalions of paratroopers sent to the Falklands. Cooper related a nocturnal experience during the British assault on Argentinian positions at Goose Green.

'The snipers tried to help out where the companies were being held up. On one occasion we had to move quickly when we came under anti-aircraft fire. We'd obviously been seen and had to move back into dead ground fairly nimbly. Although the ground was open, it did give us quite a lot of scope for movement in dead ground, until you were within range. Then it was a question of suppressing fire, while the companies or platoons moved. That amounted to putting down harassing fire into the Argentine bunkers.

'In one incident when I called the wind, the sniper fired and a white flag appeared out of the bunker, which was a good 600–700 metres [656–766 yards] away. On the shooting range the signal for a miss is a white and red flag, and the sniper made the comment that they were signalling a wash-out. Clearly, the Argentines were unhappy about the rounds going through the slots in their bunkers, but there was not a lot we could do when someone [640m] 700 yards away wants to surrender.'

OPERATION DESERT STORM

Nearly a decade after the reclamation of the Falklands by the British, war erupted in the Middle East. On 2 August 1990, Iraqi dictator Saddam Hussein ordered his army, on paper one of the most formidable in the world, to invade the neighbouring Arab nation of Kuwait. The Iraqi army had fought a bloody, protracted war with Iran during the 1980s, and some of its soldiers were combat experienced. Others, it was later proven, had been impressed into the service at gunpoint.

> ### DEADLY ACCURACY
>
> 'The British were impressed with the determination of the Argentinian snipers, who caused many casualties. During the attack on Mount Longdon, an entire British company was held up for hours by a single Argentinian sniper. "Men found themselves being hit more than once by the same sniper", wrote one British officer, "a terrifying tribute to the accuracy of the Argentinian's fire".'
>
> Adrian Gilbert,
> *Stalk and Kill: The Sniper Experience*

In response to the Iraqi aggression, a US-led coalition undertook an extensive military build-up in the region, which came to be known as Operation Desert Shield. The fighting forces of many nations took part in the liberation of Kuwait, which commenced with a massive air bombardment of military targets in Iraq on 17 January 1991. Iraqi forces attempted one incursion at the town of Khafji, just across the border with Saudi Arabia, and following a sharp clash the invaders were killed, captured, or driven back across the border. Iraqi sniper fire proved hazardous, but troops from Saudi Arabia and Qatar, supported by US Marines, eliminated holdout snipers during several days of fighting.

A month after the beginning of the air campaign, Coalition forces launched the ground phase of what was now termed Operation Desert Storm. After approximately 100 hours of rapid movement and engagement of any Iraqi forces which offered resistance, the army of Saddam Hussein was routed and in full retreat. Although the ground phase of Desert Storm was swiftly successful, Coalition forces engaged in the elimination of Iraqi snipers, efforts to establish security and the

Above: *Armed with an M-40A1 sniper rifle and accompanied by an observer, a US Marine sniper takes position during Operation Desert Shield, 1991.*

destruction of weapons caches. Author Mark Welch described some activities of Company K, Third Battalion, 5th Marine Regiment, during Desert Storm.

'The Al Wafrah forest was an area with several low trees, small farms, agriculture and livestock plots, homes, and a small town … The Al Wafrah oilfields were not too far away,' he noted. 'The minefields had been under the watchful eyes of Marine Snipers throughout the night. Every now & then the Snipers would fire a round and take out an enemy soldier in one of the many bunkers.…'

Modern sniper rifles continue to evolve as a result of improved technology, computer-aided design, feedback from the battlefield, and enhancements such as the latest generation of thermal and infrared sights. During Desert Storm and beyond, the US Army has primarily outfitted its snipers with the 7.62mm (0.30in) M-24 rifle, which builds upon the older Winchester Model 700 design. In 1996, the US Marine Corps began to replace the M-40A1, also based on the Winchester Model 700, with the M-40A3. The M-24 and the M-40A models are equipped with 10-power sights and bipods for steadier firing due to weight in excess of 5.4kg (12lbs).

WEAPONRY

The standard British Army sniper rifle is the Accuracy International L96, which was introduced in the 1980s as the successor to the venerable L42. Produced in several variants, the L96 has been proven serviceable in extreme climatic conditions and is accurate up to 800m (875 yards) in its NATO configuration, with some Magnum variants accurate beyond 1100m (1203 yards). The Royal Marines employ the Accuracy International 8.59mm (0.338in) long-range rifle, also referred to as the Super Magnum. Since World War II, weapons as large as 12.7mm (0.50in) calibre have sometimes been employed in a sniping role. Most recently, advanced heavy sniper weapons have been used with devastating effect. Among the most successful are the Barrett 'Light Fifty', known to the US military as the M–82A1, and the M–107, also a 12.7mm (0.50in) long-range rifle. US snipers were reported to have dispatched targets as distant as 1600m (1750 yards) with the Barrett 'Light Fifty' during Desert Storm. Its heavy round has also been demonstrated to be effective against armoured vehicles with a skin of up to 70mm (2.75in) thickness. Hundreds of the M–107 (or XM–107), military jargon for the Barrett Model 95, are currently in service with US forces. The M–107, smaller and lighter than its predecessor, is accurate to an amazing 2000m (2187 yards).

THE WAR ON TERROR

The horrific attacks against the World Trade Center in New York and the Pentagon in Washington D.C. on 11 September 2001, signalled an escalation of the war against terror. American and British troops engaged and defeated the Iraqi Army in the field and toppled the regime of Saddam Hussein during an approximately three-week war in the spring of 2003. However, after the occupation of the capital, Baghdad, and Basra, Iraq's second-largest city, fighting with militia, guerrillas and remnants of

Left: *On the firing range, a British Royal Marine tries his hand with a sniper version of the SA80. The SA80 replaced the SLR in the mid-1980s and, despite complaints from combat troops of unreliabilty in dusty, high-temperature conditions, it remains the standard issue rifle of the British Army.*

'Firing it feels like someone slashing you on the back of your hockey helmet with a hockey stick.'

Canadian sniper on the recoil of his .50-calibre rifle

the armed forces still loyal to Saddam Hussein continued. Along with contingents from a number of other nations, US and British forces have sought to stabilize the country and facilitate a restoration of government by the Iraqi people. Prior to the war against Saddam Hussein, US and allied forces were already engaged in a fight against the oppressive Taliban regime in Afghanistan and the terrorist organization Al-Qaeda, which perpetrated the attacks of 11 September. With the Taliban deposed, a new government has been established in Afghanistan, but combat has continued as terrorists and Taliban fighters offer resistance.

The value of trained sniper forces has perhaps never been demonstrated as clearly as during the fighting in Iraq and Afghanistan. Often, terrorists and militia will use innocent people as human shields, and shooting must be deadly accurate. In 2002, during Operation Anaconda in the Afghan mountains, two teams of Canadian snipers performed brilliantly and earned recommendations for the Bronze Star medal from their US allies. Michael Smith and Chris Wattie reported for the *National Post* that the five snipers from the 3rd Battalion, Princess Patricia's Canadian Light Infantry, fought alongside the scout platoon of the US Army's 187th 'Rakkasan' Brigade for 19 days. Near an Al-Qaeda stronghold east of Gardez, the Canadians provided invaluable fire support.

'One member of the team, a corporal from Newfoundland, said on his first night in combat he and his partner got an Al-Qaeda machine gun in their sights …,' related Smith and Wattie. 'Crawling up into a good position, they set up their [12.7mm] .50-calibre rifle – the MacMillan Tac-50, a weapon the corporal compares to having superhuman power in your hands. "Firing it feels like someone slashing you on the back of your hockey helmet with a hockey stick." When he hit his first

UNDER WATCHFUL EYES

Deadly aim, delivering a lethal single shot, is the most recognized trait of the skilled sniper. However, the total sniper package includes other capabilities as well. Chief among these is the power of observation.

Working in pairs, sniper and spotter will often switch roles to avoid fatigue and strained vision. The modern sniper team, in either role, must possess a heightened sense of its surroundings. The sniper's powers of observation, particularly when using high-powered optical devices, may be critical to the outcome of an engagement. The sniper may observe enemy troop movements, fire an effective shot, and slip away with valuable intelligence. He may call in an air strike or artillery barrage with telling effect.

In modern warfare, the 'scouting' duties of a sniper are in high demand. His ability to assess a situation and make the proper decision can spell the difference between victory and defeat.

target, an enemy gunman at a distance of 1,700 metres [1859 yards], he said all that ran through his mind was locating his next target.

'A master corporal from Ontario, the lead sniper of his three-man team, said when they first landed in the combat zone "our spider senses were tingling ... It was night and we didn't know what to expect". By daylight, after coming under enemy machine-gun fire, he managed to ease his rifle barrel between two rocks and quickly located an enemy sniper hiding behind a small piece of corrugated steel between two trees. He guessed the distance at 1,700 metres [1859 yards] and fired one shot through the metal, killing the man instantly....'

The casualties inflicted on the enemy by the Canadian troops in Afghanistan were their first in combat since the Korean War. The corporal from Newfoundland delivered a fatal shot from 2430m (2657 yards) later during the fighting, a distance which is believed to be a record.

On 6 March 2004, US Special Operations snipers in Afghanistan engaged Islamic militants with telling results. *The New York Times* News Service reported, 'US Special Operations soldiers and Afghan National Army troops killed nine armed men suspected of being Islamic militants ... The firefight occurred when roughly 40 armed men tried to flank a US sniper position east of a US base ... in Patika Province.'

Above: *A member of a three-man US Army scout team employs night-vision goggles for target acquisition along an Iraqi roadway dubbed RPG Alley. Effective night-vision equipment gave the Coalition forces a significant advantage over Iraqi forces in the 2003 war.*

Right: In April 2003, during Operation Iraqi Freedom, a British sniper team armed with an Accuracy International L96 rifle scans the distance for enemy personnel in Al Zubayr, southern Iraq.

IRAQI FREEDOM

Prior to the initiation of overt offensive operations during Operation Iraqi Freedom, men of the Central Intelligence Agency's (CIA) paramilitary division and Special Operations forces were on the ground in enemy territory. According to reporter Dana Priest of the *Washington Post*, snipers and demolitions experts were hunting Saddam Hussein, high-ranking members of his ruling Ba'ath Party and commanders of the Iraqi Army's elite Republican Guard. 'The covert teams are just one feature of the largely invisible war being waged in Iraq by the CIA's and Pentagon's growing covert paramilitary and special operations divisions,' reported Priest on 31 March 2003. 'CIA units and special operations teams are also involved in organising tribal groups to fight the Iraqi government from the north ... The teams carry sophisticated weapons and communications equipment capable of receiving near real-time targeting intelligence to guide them to locations where sought-after individuals are located.'

The very nature of the sniper's craft is covert, and in Iraq these activities have taken novel forms. Among these is the deployment of five teams of 10 airborne snipers which are tasked with defending the country's northern oil pipeline from sabotage. According to ABC News, UH-60 Blackhawk helicopters were modified to carry snipers of the elite Tiger Force, who remain airborne over the pipeline and close rapidly with suspected saboteurs. The snipers carry both the M-107 0.50in (12.7mm) calibre rifle and smaller bolt-action weapons for closer targets.

'It's the same system we used in Vietnam and we've brought it out of retirement,' explained Sergeant Brian Stinson, a sniper with the 101st Airborne Division. 'There is so much area to cover that it requires precision fire; we're on call for 24 hours a day and can be airborne within 30 minutes. We can hit a target before it knows we're there.'

In an urban setting, confronted by an enemy who wears no uniform, the need for accurate rifle fire is magnified. Lieutenant Colonel Ben Curry of Royal Marine 3 Commando Brigade told the BBC that operations conducted by his unit and US Marines under British command in and around the southern port city of Umm Qasr had been complicated by members of the Iraqi military firing a few shots, throwing their uniforms away and then melting into the civilian population. Control of the streets is key to the prevention of a descent into chaos, and a group of Iraqi arms dealers violated the law in the town of Tikrit with dire consequences.

'US Army snipers shot and killed two Iraqis and injured three others today at a market here in what military spokesmen said was an operation aimed at breaking up an arms bazaar,' said *Washington Post* writer Theola Labbé in August 2003. 'Acting on reports that weapons were being sold openly every Friday, military officials posted ambush teams from the 4th Infantry Division's 1st Battalion, 22nd Infantry Regiment on rooftops above a marketplace in the center of this city northwest of Baghdad, the spokesmen said. After five hours of surveillance, the snipers saw a red

Below: From a rooftop lookout, a US Marine uses a spotting telescope to scan for an Iraqi sniper, shortly after a rocket-propelled grenade attack near the city of Fallujah, March 2004. Snipers were used in a counter-insurgency role in Iraq.

car pull up at 7:22 a.m. Two men got out, each holding an AK–47.... The men pulled empty rice sacks out of the car, laid them on the ground and covered them with thousands of 7.62mm [0.30in] bullets, electrical wires and other ordnance.'

An American officer explained that according to the rules of engagement issued to US forces any armed person was considered hostile. One of the dead was reported to have been carrying an identification card which linked him to the former regime as a 'Friend of Saddam'. The card was said to have allowed him to visit the dictator once a year, for his children to receive special privileges in school and for him to receive an annual bonus.

HEAVY WEAPONS

The awesome power of the heavy sniper weapons used in Iraq is graphically illustrated in a report by Lieutenant Colonel Jim Smith released in May 2003. A sniper of the 325th Parachute Infantry Regiment detailed the action.

Below: An Iraqi militiaman holds an AK series assault rifle with a sniper scope near the shrine of Imam Ali in the Holy city of Najaf, April 2004.

IRAQ: RULES OF ENGAGEMENT

In September 2003, Lieutenant General Ricardo Sanchez, commander of US Combined Joint Task Force 7 in Iraq, told the media that combat troops under his command were well trained to obey established rules of engagement.

'My soldiers on the ground every day are making decisions to engage or not engage, and to capture or kill people based on the circumstances,' the general said to the American Forces Press Service. 'Whenever we are engaged, or we feel there is a self-defense threat, we will respond with the necessary level of force.'

Concerning the enforcement of checkpoints, US troops were instructed to fire warning shots before using deadly force. While on patrol in Iraqi cities, soldiers were authorized to shoot to kill when confronted. If attacked, Sanchez warned, sufficient combat power would be brought to bear against the enemy to eliminate the threat.

'The Barrett [12.7mm] .50-cal. sniper rifle may have been the most useful piece of equipment for the urban fight – especially for our light fighters,' acknowledged Smith. 'The XM107 was used to engage both vehicular and personnel targets out to 1,400 meters [1531 yards]. Soldiers not only appreciated the range and accuracy but also the target effect. Leaders and scouts viewed the effect of the [12.7mm] .50-cal. round as a combat multiplier due to the psychological impact on other combatants that viewed the destruction of the target.'

Insurgents and guerrilla fighters have employed hit-and-run tactics, roadside bombs and mostly ineffective sniper fire against US, British and other Coalition troops during Operation Iraqi Freedom. On one occasion north of Baghdad, the Associated Press said, the militiamen even released pigeons as a signal to initiate an ambush. The attackers, however, got the worst of the engagement as 11 were killed. US snipers had been located in key positions and took their toll on the enemy without striking any civilians.

In the near future, it may become even more difficult for insurgents and guerrillas to hide. If captured, they may be tested with a RIFF kit, which NBC News says provides a chemical process to determine whether an individual has fired a weapon within 48 hours of the test. Skin or clothing can be chemically swabbed for gunpowder residue, and if the swab turns blue the Coalition forces may have removed one more enemy combatant from the streets.

STREET FIGHTING

Even for the trained sniper, the unpredictable nature of guerrilla warfare in an urban setting can present significant challenges. Some would say, the ultimate challenge. Members of Fox Company, Battalion Landing Team, 2nd Battalion, 2nd Marines,

24th Marine Expeditionary Force, were ordered to recover the body of a comrade killed in a convoy ambush earlier. The assignment was completed, but not before the unit's snipers had been called in to quell resistance.

'The first attempt was thwarted when a group of armed Iraqis with small arms fired on the approaching Marines and a firefight ensued,' wrote Corporal Jeff Sisto. 'During the engagement, Marine scout snipers had one confirmed kill at 1,000 meters [1094 yards]. From a rooftop, snipers observed an adult male armed with an AK-47 assault rifle hiding behind the corner of a building and grasping the shoulder of a child in front of him as a shield.

"'I shot 3 to 4 feet away from him on the face of the building, which made the kid run away and the man come out to inspect the impact", said one of the scout snipers from Surveillance Target and Acquisition platoon. "That is when my team member shot the armed individual in the chest".'

In order to facilitate the training of sniper candidates, the US Army Sniper Training School at Fort Benning, Georgia, dispatched three sniper instructors and a mobile training team (MTT) to Baghdad, where they began training 20 selected individuals of the 1st Armored Division, according to a report from the 372nd Mobile Public Affairs Detachment. The prime motivation for sending the MTT to Iraq was to assist in coping with the Iraqi desert terrain and conditions, which are quite different from those at Fort Benning. Rather than the standard five weeks, the mobile course is one week shorter, but the instructors assert that the soldiers are in a combat frame of mind in Iraq and thus easier to train. The snipers practised on targets plastered with the likenesses of the 55 most wanted high-ranking Iraqi fugitives and learned valuable techniques for intelligence-gathering, observation and effectively calling in air and artillery support when necessary.

DEVASTATING IMPACT

"'My spotter positively identified a target at 1,400 meters [1531 yards] carrying an RPG on a water tower," said the sniper.
"I engaged the target. The top half of the torso fell forward out of the tower and the lower portion remained in the tower." There were other personal anecdotes of one round destroying two targets and another of the target "disintegrating".'

Lt Colonel Smith, 325th Parachute Infantry Regiment, on hitting a target with a Tac-50

LETHAL COMBINATION

In wartime, the tactical advantage most often turns toward the side whose troops are the most highly trained and motivated and best equipped. The accomplished sniper brings all three elements together in a lethal combination. Building by building and block by block, snipers asserted control of vast areas of Baghdad. Ray Quintanilla of the *Chicago Tribune* talked with two snipers who had been sent on a mission to silence an enemy machine gun in the spring of 2003.

'The pop, pop, pop of sporadic gunfire has drawn the attention of Sgts. Daniel Osborne and Cyrus Field,' said Quintanilla. 'Responding to persistent Iraqi attacks on a nearby US military compound, the US Army snipers have taken positions on

Opposite: *Lance Sergeant Chris Briggs, serving as a sniper with the 1st Battalion, Irish Guards, takes up position close to the city of Basra, southern Iraq, April 2003. Briggs was in one of four sniper pairs set up to provide covering fire for the Royal Engineers attempting to put out one of the numerous oil well fires.*

the roof of a nearby abandoned building to sit and wait for the right moment to lock onto their target. For them and other sniper teams now prowling Baghdad streets, a successful mission often ends with a ferocious craaaaack! And so it would be on this night.

'A short time after Osborne and Field set up on the roof, the hostile gunfire on the ground is interrupted by four thunderous blasts. Then there is only silence. "That's a confirmed kill!" a voice on one of the men's radios exclaims as the snipers sit on the roof scanning the streets below. "That's the fourth one tonight!" ...

'The battle is now being waged from rooftops and other vantage points against isolated attacks on US troops. The enemy is no longer a conventional Iraqi soldier. It's one who has chosen to strike under cover of darkness.

'American forces have responded to the threat in recent days by unleashing dozens of sniper teams all across Baghdad – such as Osborne and Field – to thwart those attacks. Their standing order: Shoot to kill anyone who fires on US troops or equipment. In the last two weeks, this team alone has recorded more than 20 enemy kills.

'"All day, you build up for the moment when you fire the shot", Field, 23, says as he and his partner take positions in a hostile zone. "Then there's a feeling of exhilaration, and you feel like you've really done something for your country. You've taken someone out ..."

'And on this night, with loaded weapons strapped to their backs, the two men sidestep piles of garbage to climb a dark and musty stairwell before finding "the right

ROOFTOP ACTION

At a distance of 300m (328 yards), Sergeant Randall Davis of the US Army's Stryker Brigade registered his eighth kill in the Iraqi town of Samarra. Matthew Cox recorded the drama of the event for the *Army Times*. '"It was just getting dark. I saw a guy step in front of the light", said the 25-year-old sniper. Davis knew he was watching another sniper by the way the man stepped back into the shadows and crept along the roofline to spy down on a squad from his unit – B Company, 5th Battalion, 20th Infantry Regiment ...

'From his own rooftop position, Davis tracked him with his favorite weapon – an M-14 rifle equipped with a special sight that has crosshairs and a red aiming dot. He didn't have to wait long before the enemy sniper made his second mistake.

'"He silhouetted his rifle from the waist up, trying to look over at the guys in the courtyard", Davis said. His M-14 spoke once. "I hit him in the chest. He fell back. His rifle flew out of his hands ..." Confirmed kill, his eighth – which includes seven enemies picked off in one day.'

The Iraqi sniper, who had been carrying a Russian 7.62mm (0.30in) Dragunov SVD sniper rifle, would undoubtedly have opened fire on Davis's comrades only moments later. One shot – one kill. An enemy falls, and the life of a friend has been saved. Stealthy and silent, then suddenly violent ... such is the war of the sniper.

spot" on top of a four-storey building. They are here to find a group of Iraqi men firing shots at a nearby US military compound the last few nights … Lt. Col. Jeff Ingram of the 2-70th Armored Battalion instructed the snipers two nights earlier to track the men, who are firing a [12.7mm] .50-caliber machine gun …

'A few minutes past midnight, they hear the familiar sounds of a [12.7mm] .50-caliber machine gun firing short bursts near a clump of trees [732m] 800 yards away … Within 30 seconds, the snipers are in position. One rifle is mounted on a bipod. The other rests over the building's ledge. There are no second thoughts about firing, the men say … Their green-image night-vision scope reveals four men standing around a machine gun. Each one is no bigger than the head of a pin from such a great distance …

'Within 10 seconds, Field and Osborne fire four shots. Two rounds are fired simultaneously. Sparks and flames are thrust out of the gun's barrel as the trigger is pulled … Two Iraqi men are hit while standing next to the gun. The two others are struck while trying to run. In just a few seconds, four Iraqis are face down within [4.6m] 15 feet of one another …'

Such encounters, brief but savage, are the true test of the sniper's training, tactics and fortitude. The ability to target an enemy combatant, then pull the trigger with detached professionalism is a skill set which must be honed to a razor's edge. A moment's hesitation may mean the difference between life and death – for he who is sighting may well be simultaneously sighted.

Above: *A sniper of the US Army's 25th Division sights his M-24 rifle in the direction of hostile fire during fighting near the Shiite Muslim holy city of Najaf, April 2004.*

At the cutting edge of weapons technology, the AN/PAS-13 Thermal Weapon Sight, a high-tech infrared device which can be adapted to small arms, is now in use with various armed forces. Here, a US soldier undergoes training in the use of this complicated and expensive piece of equipment.

CHAPTER TEN

MODERN SNIPERS

Major military organizations worldwide, firmly committed to highly trained, specialized sniper forces, rely on these élite professionals for the same reasons as their predecessors. The modern sniper eliminates high-value targets, undermines enemy morale and gathers intelligence.

Throughout its history, the military craft of the sniper has been at times highly valued, while at others it has been deemed an unnecessary expense. The sniper himself has been seen both as a hero and a pariah. During times of war and peace, the demand for the sniper's services has ebbed and flowed. In recent years, however, the commanders of modern armies have come to the realization that a well-trained sniper is an invaluable asset on the battlefield.

Subsequently, the formalization of sniper training and the refinement of his equipment have followed. Given the nature of the sniper's combat role, it is obvious that even the best of soldiers may not be suited for such duty. The sniper résumé includes multiple qualifications. Being a crack shot is only part of the total package.

SNIPER TRAINING

Major sniper training courses are extremely rigorous and of several weeks' duration. Various sniper training programmes, both military and paramilitary, exist around the world. The most prominent of these are the US Marine Corps Scout Sniper training programme, the US Army Sniper School, and the British Royal Marine sniper training programme. Graduates of these comprehensive courses are masters in marksmanship, camouflage and concealment, observation, intelligence gathering and survival.

The demand for qualified snipers is on the increase, primarily due to the nature of modern armed conflict. The general definition of the sniper is one who is capable of concealing himself from the enemy, firing a weapon with precision in order to inflict casualties on high-value targets, gather intelligence and withdraw unharmed. The use of an accurately telescopic-sighted bolt-action rifle is often preferable to a weapon which ejects a spent cartridge automatically due to the fact that a piece of flying metal might attract attention. He may also carry a conventional rifle for close combat, and possibly sophisticated night vision gear.

PAIRED UP

The military doctrine of most major armed forces dictates that snipers operate in pairs, shooter and observer. This team may often swap roles to lessen fatigue and eye strain as much as possible. Snipers are trained in appropriate methods of movement across the battlefield, whether urban, arctic, desert or jungle. They are proficient in digging a 'hide' or nest from which to operate and are schooled in sketching the field before them to identify positions where targets may appear. Such identification facilitates communication between shooter and observer.

The ghillie suit, first employed by Scottish gamekeepers, has become an integral part of the sniper's accoutrements. The suit is usually made by the sniper himself and consists of a pair of overalls or a jumpsuit covered with mesh and then festooned with natural or manmade camouflage, such as local vegetation and strips of earth-toned canvas which help to break up a silhouette.

A sniper's hood completes the suit and usually includes a mesh veil which covers the face and sometimes the muzzle of the rifle. Snipers are further trained to recognize the appropriate level of response to a given situation. A single shot may be the optimum offensive action; however, calling in artillery or an air strike may produce better results.

'Military snipers traditionally have struggled to defend their image in the public

SNIPER QUALITIES

The soldier who aspires to the sniper designation must possess a number of outstanding traits. In *Sniper*, author Adrian Gilbert discusses some of the basic qualities needed.

'The first of the specific qualities and skills required of a sniper is expertise in marksmanship, preferably demonstrated by high scores in shooting contests or qualification as an expert marksman,' writes Gilbert. 'Good physical condition is also necessary, as extended operations require the sniper to go without sleep, food or water for long periods. He needs good hearing and excellent, unaided vision; the wearing of glasses is a liability, as the lenses can reflect sunlight and loss or breakage would render the sniper ineffectual. Smokers are discouraged: smoking on a mission makes the sniper vulnerable to detection, while to refrain can lead to nervousness and irritation, thereby lowering efficiency.

'Mentally, the sniper needs intelligence, initiative, common sense and patience. On the training course, he has to master a wide and often disparate body of knowledge, and in combat he must be able to apply this information swiftly and correctly. Lastly, the sniper must be a mature personality who is able to cope with the stress of calculated, deliberate killing.'

eye,' wrote Roxana Tiron for *National Defense Magazine*. "Some people think that we are the sneaky guys who just go out and indiscriminately kill", said Master Sgt. Mark Carey, an instructor at the [US] Special Warfare Training Group at Fort Bragg, N.C. The reality is that, "in the military, we talk discipline and controlled fire", he said … "You do not want a power shooter". The soldiers selected are "above-average intelligence for the most part; they are independent, self-disciplined; they have to demonstrate marksmanship ability and field craft skills, and they have to be cleared by a Defense Department psychiatrist …".'

According to Tiron, the US Army Rangers are in the process of adding 26 more snipers to each battalion, a significant increase on the existing standard of 14.

BRITISH ARMY SNIPER TRAINING

The oldest active sniper training programme is that of the Royal Marines. For many, it was this military organization which primarily maintained the standards and curriculum necessary to keep sniper skills alive. The nine-week course, at Lympstone in Devon, is attended by candidates who are typically three-year military veterans. They must demonstrate their proficiency with the rifle at 600m (656 yards) or more,

Above: Wearing adapted ghillie suits, a US Marine sniper team looks down range, training with a M-82A1 .50-calibre (12.7mm) sniper rifle at Camp Pendleton, California.

Right: *Russian private
Yevgeny Romanenko,
from the Tomsk region,
takes up a firing
position at the
approaches to
Gudermes, a town on
the Russia–Chechnya
border, November 1999.
He is armed with the
standard Russian army
sniper rifle, the
Dragunov SVD.*

conceal themselves within 250m (273 yards) of an observer and fire a blank round, stalk a distance of up to 1000m (1093 yards) and again successfully fire a blank round at an 'enemy' position, judge distances accurately, and pass a written examination.

During the fieldcraft portion of the course, the candidate, using his telescopic sight, must locate seven of 10 items of military equipment concealed about an open field. A time limit of 40 minutes to complete this exercise is strictly enforced. Over the nine weeks, the candidate may participate in as many as 18 stalks. Two successive 'shots' from an undetected position earn the candidate his sniper badge and qualify him for deployment. The failure rate for this rigorous course is 50 per cent.

The British Joint Sniper Training Establishment (JSTE) also conducts a sniper programme at Sennybridge, Wales, which is mainly attended by Royal Air Force, Royal Navy and Army personnel. Six weeks long, the JSTE course is similar to that of the Royal Marines, incorporating basic concepts such as stalking, construction of a 'hide', forward observation training for aircraft and artillery, and communications.

MARINE CORPS SNIPER SCHOOL

Drawing upon the extensive successes of their snipers during the Vietnam War, the United States Marine Corps established a permanent sniper school at Quantico, Virginia, in 1977. Major Jim Land, well known for training snipers in Vietnam, commanded the school along with Major Dick Culver. Sergeant Carlos Hathcock, a sniper legend, was the first noncommissioned officer in charge (NCOIC). The Marines have also established an eastern school at Camp LeJeune, North Carolina, and a western school at Camp Pendleton, California. The course is similar in many respects to that of the Royal Marines, and its failure rate is roughly 30 per cent. The basic US Marine scout-sniper course is 10 weeks long and consists of three phases, an academic package and range shooting, fieldcraft in which the students make their ghillie suits, and stalking.

The US 3rd Marine Division was the first to actively train snipers in Vietnam, and the formation maintains a scout-sniper school at Kaneohe Bay on the Hawaiian island of Oahu. 'The Marine Corps has the best sniper program in the world,' Gunnery Sergeant Richard Tisdale, the school's NCOIC, told the Marine Corps

GOOD NEIGHBOUR POLICY

In a given year, the military forces of nations around the world may send contingents to sniper school in the United States or Great Britain. NATO allies such as Belgium, the Netherlands and Norway have regularly taken advantage of such cooperative opportunities. In addition, a longstanding exchange programme continues between the British and American services. At times, trained snipers and instructors take their show on the road, participating in joint exercises in Central America, the Middle East and Asia.

The perception of the sniper's role in combat, however, may vary in some instances. According to author Adrian Gilbert in *Sniper*, the British and US philosophy places the sniper in support of regular infantry units without being formally attached to them. Such an arrangement permits greater freedom of movement. Other armies, such as the French, Israeli and Russian, assign snipers directly to infantry units. While in theory this may broaden the range of the regular soldier, it may simultaneously restrict the sniper's movement.

Right: *Hiding and waiting, a US Army Special Forces sniper makes the most of cover and concealment. Most snipers fashion their own camouflage ghillie suits.*

News Service. 'When many people think of a sniper, they think of a person who randomly shoots people. A sniper selects his target and fires upon it.... We train our snipers to be patient and wait for the perfect opportunity to fire upon the target when it will best support the mission. They could lay in a dormant position for days at a time before actually pulling the trigger and engaging on the target.'

US ARMY SNIPERS

The US Army sniper school was formally established at Fort Benning, near Columbus, Georgia, in 1987. During the conflict in Iraq, elements of the Fort Benning cadre have deployed to that country to conduct sniper training under desert conditions, which cannot be replicated in the southeastern United States. The standard course is five weeks long, and candidates must qualify for admission with proficiency in marksmanship, physical training and intelligence gathering. They must also have 20/20 vision, without colour blindness, and may be required to submit to a psychological evaluation. A sniper assessment programme, which allows Army personnel to qualify for the sniper school at Fort Benning, is currently operating at Fort Lewis, Washington.

Gilbert relates that the Army programme is 'necessarily more limited in scope than that taught by the Marines, but it none the less trains its students to engage targets with precision fire at ranges out to a thousand metres [1093 yards] and to be proficient in fieldcraft. The school is run by the 29th Infantry Regiment, and training is demanding, with every moment of the student's time taken up with work.

'Captain Mark L. Rozycki, who was responsible for the operation and administration of the school in the late 1980s made these notes on the running of the course: "Training during the first week is oriented on fieldcraft techniques, sniper patrol orders, and sniper movement techniques. The students also zero their

Below: A member of a contingent of US forces deployed to restore order in Haiti in 1994, this sniper aims his bolt-action rifle toward the scene of a disturbance.

weapons and receive training on marksmanship fundamentals. They spend an average of four hours a night constructing their ghillie suits, writing their first patrol order, and studying. Cadre members are available to help them. Throughout the second week, the soldiers participate in a number of evaluated exercises that include their first record fire, concealed movement, and target designation. To facilitate training, the sniper class is divided into two training groups but with the members of each sniper team kept together. On the eighth day, the training moves out of the classroom to the range and the fieldcraft training sites....'"

Carrying the explicit need for sniper training to a more pervasive level in the US military, a National Guard sniper school was established at Camp Robinson, near Little Rock, Arkansas, in 1993. Given the high levels of National Guard and Reserve troops deployed to Iraq, this training has been fortuitous. National Guardsmen train for two weeks and then return for a second two-seek round within the same year. During one class, the Department of Defense Press reported, 11 of an initial 21 students successfully completed their first two-week stint.

Minimum requirements for the National Guard course include a score of 70 per cent on a physical training test, a demonstrated ability to estimate the range to a target and hits on 14 of 20 targets from distances between 300 and 600m (328 to 650 yards). 'The intensity of the training is the same as it is at Benning,' instructor Sergeant Tom Dow told the Department of Defense. 'These Guard people put in the same number of hours and days during their two-week phases as we do in five straight weeks. We take the weekends off. They don't.'

SNIPER SCHOOLS OF THE WORLD

Only a handful of snipers are fielded by the Canadian military; however, their record during the fighting against the Al-Qaeda and Taliban terrorist organizations in Afghanistan was impressive. Canadian snipers are trained at the Combat Training Centre at the Gagetown base in the province of New Brunswick. The government of the Philippines is engaged in an ongoing struggle against paramilitary guerrilla elements. Since 1967, the Philippine Marine Corps has operated a scout-sniper school similar to the US Marine programme.

The world's premier sniper schools participate in exchange programmes and train personnel from other domestic military organizations, as well as candidates from other countries. Members of the British Special Air Service, a covert operations group, may qualify as snipers at the Royal Marine school. US Special Forces and Navy SEAL (Sea, Air and Land) students participate in the Army and Marine courses. An elite counter-sniper unit of the US Air Force has also trained at Camp Robinson in Arkansas. The School of the Americas, located at Fort Benning, conducts training for up to 2000 soldiers per year from various Latin American countries, and that training includes a sniper course.

At various times, forces will engage in joint exercises. During a 10-day period

RUSSIAN SNIPER TRAINING

Following several years of stagnation and notable setbacks during the Chechen Wars, the Russian Army established a sniper school in the summer of 1999. However, traditional sniper doctrine continued to produce disappointing results until fundamental tactics were changed and Russian snipers began to operate in two- or three-man hunter-killer detachments, say authors Lester W. Grau and Charles Q. Cutshaw in *Infantry Magazine*. An elite group of professional Russian snipers has emerged in recent years, who use the Dragunov 7.62mm (0.30in) sniper rifle (see picture). The training of these individuals, who are usually under the jurisdiction of the Ministry of the Interior or the FSB, the successor to the Soviet KGB intelligence organization, takes place at a facility near Moscow.

M82A1 BARRETT 'LIGHT FIFTY'

Country of Origin	United States
Calibre	0.5in (12.7mm)
Overall length	1448mm (57in)
Barrel length	737mm (29in)
Weight	12.9kg (28.3lb)

several years ago, US Marines and troops of the Japan Ground Self-Defense Force (JGSDF) participated in 'Forest Light 99' in the Kirishima Mountains of Japan.

'A platoon of 1st Lt. [Takanobu] Fukakusa's soldiers spent the morning together with a platoon of Marine snipers practicing stalking and observation techniques,' reported US Marine Sergeant Matt Hevezi. 'The snipers paired up with Japanese soldiers and helped them don special camouflage uniforms used by US Marine snipers. In teams of two, the snipers and soldiers scattered into the surrounding hills and underbrush before attempting to creep within shooting range of an observation team. The mission was to move in together for an accurate shot without being spotted by observers equipped with high-powered binoculars.'

The Japanese officer added, 'It is a pleasure to train with Marines because we can learn their battle skills. I study your camouflage methods, how your Marines move, and especially how your scouts think. The learning between the US Marines and Japanese soldiers is very fine.'

EQUIPMENT

To some extent, the firearms used by snipers are a matter of personal preference. The venerable M-14 rifle with telescopic sights has been utilized by US forces as recently as the fighting in Iraq and Afghanistan. The basic design of the Remington 700 has been enhanced in the M-24 sniper weapons system now issued by the US Army. Remington cites the weapon's 'out of the box' accuracy as a prime advantage over other systems. The rifle also uses a heavy stainless steel barrel and fibreglass stock. It fires the NATO 7.62mm (0.30in) cartridge, can be used with a detachable bipod and is often equipped with 10-power telescopic sights. The primary US Marine sniper rifle, designated the M-40A3, is also based on the Remington 700, with its floorplate assembly and trigger guard being built by the D.D. Ross Company. The M-40A3, which began replacing the older M-40A1 in 1996, also fires the NATO 7.62mm (0.30in) cartridge, and can be used with a bipod. Typically, the M-40A3 is equipped with a Unertl 10-power telescopic sight.

The 0.50in (12.7mm) calibre M82A1 Barrett 'Light Fifty' was supplied to American snipers during Operation Desert Storm and allowed them to engage targets at up to 1500m (1640 yards). Weighing 12.9kg (28.3lbs) and usually equipped with a 10-power telescopic sight, the M82A1 also employs a 10-round ammunition clip. Another 0.50in (12.7mm) calibre sniper rifle which became a favourite during the Gulf War is the Research Armament Industries M500, which is accurate to 1800m (1969 yards). The semiautomatic Barrett M-107 is the latest generation of the big 'fifties'. The compact bullpup design of the M-107 allows it to be operated by one man and fired from the shoulder.

Below: *A US Army sniper trains with a telescopic sight fitted atop a heavy .50-calibre (12.7mm) machine gun set to function in a single shot role against distant enemy personnel.*

Manufactured by Accuracy International, the L96A1 sniper rifle system is the primary weapon of British Army and Royal Marine snipers. Firing the 7.62mm (0.30in) NATO cartridge, the bolt-action rifle is fitted with 6X42 Schmidt and Bender telescopic sights. The L96A1 went into production in 1990 as an upgrade to the original L96, which was issued to the British armed forces in the mid-1980s. An improved bolt allows the sniper to remain on target longer while chambering a fresh round, and an anti-icing system permits the rifle to function at temperatures as low as minus 40 degrees Celsius (minus 40 degrees Fahrenheit). An adjustable trigger and free-floating stainless steel barrel improve accuracy, while the weapon is also equipped with a bipod.

The Russian armed forces are continuing to research sniper rifle design, and at present their snipers continue to use mostly Soviet-era weaponry such as the Dragunov SVD rifle, which fires a 7.62mm (0.30in) cartridge from a 10-round magazine. Introduced in the late 1950s to replace the antiquated Moisin Nagant Model 1891/30 sniper rifle, the Dragunov SVD has seen service in Afghanistan and

Below: Camouflaged in full ghillie suits, a sniper team from the 2nd Battalion, the Parachute Regiment, waits for a firing opportunity with its L96A1 7.62mm (0.30in) Accuracy International sniper rifle.

Chechnya. It is normally sighted with a PSO 4X24 scope. Another Russian sniper weapon is the silenced VSS Vintorez special sniper rifle, which fires subsonic 9mm (0.35in) ammunition.

In addition to his weapon, a completely outfitted sniper may also carry binoculars, a range finder, a small knife, a digging tool for the preparation of his 'hide', a radio, a spotting telescope such as the US 20-power M49, or a periscope. A recent innovation is the tick suit, which is utilized in response to sophisticated infrared detection devices. At night, body temperature can betray a sniper's location regardless of his camouflage. State-of-the-art thermal imaging equipment, however, may be thwarted by infrared-proof tick suits, which can break up the image on a scope. A variety of night scopes and night-vision goggles are becoming more common on the battlefield.

EFFECTIVE DEPLOYMENT

The acid test of the benefits of an ongoing training programme is the effective deployment of the sniper in a combat situation. While the philosophies of military commanders may vary somewhat, modern experience has served to reinforce the contention that a sniper is a valuable asset.

On the flanks of an advancing force, snipers may provide harassing fire against an enemy, eliminating high-value targets such as officers, operators of heavier weapons such as machine guns or mortars, or enemy snipers. Counter-sniper activities and the establishment of a secure perimeter will allow friendly troops to move about without fear of being shot by an unseen foe. In a defensive role, snipers may serve as a screen for the rearguard, slowing the progress of an enemy. In the case of inexperienced troops whose officers have been killed or wounded by accurate sniper fire, an enemy unit may be stopped cold for a lengthy period.

Snipers are capable of demoralizing the enemy, rendering him leaderless, inflicting serious casualties and relaying vital intelligence to commanders in the field. Using heavy-calibre sniper weapons, they may even disable vehicles or render a jet engine inoperable. Simply the knowledge that snipers are present may serve as a deterrent to offensive action on the part of an enemy. For more than 200 years, from the flintlock rifle to the refined technology of the twenty-first century, the trained military sniper has influenced the outcome of armed conflict. A enigmatic professional, he is a calculating and efficient executioner. Both an anachronism of the more primitive past and a symbol of the modern military, the sniper is a shadowy, unseen, constant threat. While the effectiveness of some weapons systems may wane during wars of the future, the decisive impact of a single, well-placed shot will remain.

BIBLIOGRAPHY

Asprey, Robert B. *War In The Shadows: The Guerrilla In History*. New York: William Morrow and Company, Inc., 1994.

Astor, Gerald. *June 6, 1944: the Voices of D-Day*. New York: St. Martin's Press, 1994.

Blumenson, Martin (Ed: Time-Life Books). *World War II: Liberation*. Alexandria, Virginia: Time-Life Books, 1978.

Bourke, Joanna. *An Intimate History of Killing*. New York: Basic Books, 1999.

Brookesmith, Peter. *Sniper*. Staplehurst, UK: Spellmount Ltd, 2000.

Bull, Dr. Stephen. *World War I Trench Warfare (1) 1914–16*. Oxford: Osprey Publishing, 2002.

—. *World War I Trench Warfare (2) 1916–18*. Oxford: Osprey Publishing, 2002.

Carney, John T. Jr. and Benjamin F. Schemmer. *No Room for Error: the Covert Operations of America's Special Tactics Units from Iran to Afghanistan*. New York: Ballantine Books, 2002.

Craig, William. *Enemy At The Gates: The Battle For Stalingrad*. New York: Barnes & Noble Books, 2003.

Editors of the Century Company. *Battles and Leaders of the Civil War*. New York: The Century Company, 1983.

Frankel, Stanley. *Frankel-y Speaking About World War II in the South Pacific*. Washington, D.C.: Infantry Journal Press, 1949.

Furgurson, Ernest B. *Chancellorsville 1863: The Souls of the Brave*. New York: Vintage Books, 1993.

✓ Gilbert, Adrian. *Sniper*. New York: St. Martin's Press, 1994.

—. *Stalk and Kill: The Sniper Experience*. New York: St. Martin's Press, 1997.

Hallas, James H. *The Devil's Anvil: The Assault On Peleliu*. Westport, Connecticut: Praeger Publishers, 1994.

✓ Henderson, Charles. *Marine Sniper – 93 Confirmed Kills*. New York: Berkely Books, 1986.

Higginbotham, Don. *Daniel Morgan, Revolutionary Rifleman*. Williamsburg, Va.: University of North Carolina Press, 1961.

Kern, Erich (translated by Paul Findlay). *Dance of Death*. London: Collins, 1951.

Leckie, Robert. *Strong Men Armed: the United States Marines against Japan*. New York: Da Capo Press, 1997.

McBride, Herbert W. *A Rifleman Went To War*. Mt. Ida, Arkansas: Lancer Militaria, 1987.

O'Connell, Robert L. *Of Arms and Men*. Oxford: Oxford University Press, 1989.

Pfanz, Harry. *Gettysburg – The First Day*. Chapel Hill, North Carolina: University of North Carolina Press, 2001.

Pyle, Ernie. *Here Is Your War*. Cleveland, Ohio: The World Publishing Company, 1943.

Pegler, Martin. *The Military Sniper Since 1914*. Oxford: Osprey Publishing, 2001.

Rush, Robert S. *US Infantryman in World War II (1): Pacific Area of Operations*. Oxford: Osprey Publishing, 2002.

✓ Sasser, Charles W. and Craig Roberts. *One Shot – One Kill*. New York: Pocket Books, 1990.

Seymour, William. *The Price of Folly: British Blunders in the War of American Independence*. London: Brassey's, 1995.

Shore, Captain Clifford. *With British Snipers to the Reich*. London: Greenhill Books, 1997.

INDEX

Page numbers in *italics* refer
to illustrations.

PICTURE CREDITS